ARCHITECTURAL DESIGN

Vol 58 No 1/2-1988

Editorial Offices: 42 Leinster Gardens, London W2 Telephone: 01-402 2141 Subscriptions: 7/8 Holland Street London W8

EDITOR
Dr Andreas C Papadakis
PRODUCTION EDITOR: Pamela Johnston DESIGNED BY: Andrea Bettella
ASSISTANT EDITOR: Natasha Edwards ADVERTISING: Sheila de Vallee SUBSCRIPTIONS MANAGER: Hedy Kraemer
CONSULTANTS: Catherine Cooke, Dennis Crompton, Terry Farrell, Kenneth Frampton
Charles Jencks, Heinrich Klotz, Leon Krier, Robert Maxwell, Demetri Porphyrios, Colin Rowe, Derek Walker

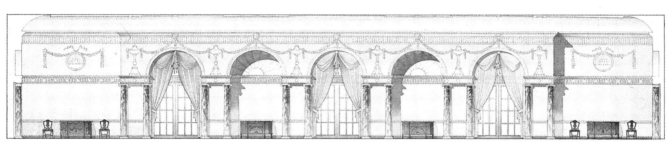

JOHN BLATTEAU, INTERIOR, US DEPARTMENT OF STATE, WASHINGTON

THE NEW CLASSICISM

Architectural Design Awards

The 1987 Architectural Design Awards continue a unique and incisive tradition that combines recognition for achievement in architecture, whether realised or theoretical, with a characteristic critical prescience that discerns the major trends and figures in architecture for years to come. A varied panel of judges comprising major critics, theorists and leading architects has established a prophetic precedent that not only recognises individual achievements but has

revealed a deep respect for theoretical content in architecture. The Awards also seek to encourage younger architects, many of whom in the past have gone on to achieve success and become leading figures – one of the most notable examples being Richard Rogers, who received his first award for his Waterfront Housing in 1964.

A further aim has been to give prominence to architects who although well established may be currently out of favour or ahead of fashion, but who have nevertheless produced distinguished work. Because *Architectural Design* is both independent and international, it has often been able to take a more robust stance in giving its awards than more parochially-minded institutions. In line with this policy, the Architectural Design Awards were extended this year to cover the full international field of architecture. Entries were by submission, but, in addition, leading editors and critics were also invited to put forward their own nominations.

Michael Graves, probably the most featured architect in *Architectural Design* acted as Chairman. The other judges were Charles Jencks, Rob Krier, Demetri Porphyrios and Andreas Papadakis. The Jury are regular contributors or consultants to *Architectural Design* and there was a certain unanimity of views and shared values, however disparate the submissions under consideration. There appeared a strong preference for figurative architecture over the abstract, and – not surprisingly – for the Post-Modern, over those of Late-Modernism or Technological baroque.

Top among the judges' choice was Jones' and Kirkland's Civic Mississauga City Hall. This is an architectural *tour de force*, not only in built form but in its encapsulation of many of the architectural conversations of the last 15 years. Its solid achieve-

ment is in demonstrating that a figurative architecture has now emerged that does not deny its debt to and its antecedence in Modernism, but is able to do what the Esperanto of Modernism was unable to do; that is, to make convincing monuments and express civic and national pride.

A major theme linking all the winning or commended schemes was an actual or implied concern with the idea of the city and the urban experience. In size, they ranged from the single family house of Duany and Plater-Zyberk to the national monument of the Indira Gandhi Centre by Ralph Lerner. In concept, they veered from the poetics of Scolari's Ark to the historical sophistication of Stirling and Venturi.

Scolari's fragmented and dissembled project, the Ark, was confined to an imaginary and Elysian ideal that conveyed the poetry of the true monument. Many of these ideas were taken up by Aldo Rossi, who in his Casa Aurora has been able to translate what may at first appear to be the mute into an urban poetry of practicality and elegance.

Gaenz and Rolfes' hospital was one of the most rewarding discoveries. This young team has provided a hospital of rare quality, both in concept and execution. Without losing any advantage that modern materials and techniques may have to offer, they have nevertheless produced a very civilised and beautiful building.

The Awards, whilst prizing the qualities of individual achievement, highlight the theoretical directions and spirit that informs current architecture and will characterise the architecture of the era. Next year's Awards are now open for submissions and nominations, which should be sent to John Melvin, Awards Secretary, *Architectural Design* Magazine, 42 Leinster Gardens, London W2. Closing date: June 30, 1988.   *John Melvin*

Jones and Kirkland: Mississauga Civic Centre, Ontario

There was little doubt in the judges minds that this was the outstanding building of this year's selection. It was admired as much for what it represented as for what it has actually achieved, both being very considerable. Firstly, it represents, in built form, 10 to 15 years of theoretical debate, paper projects and polemic. The debt to Leon Krier is clearly acknoledged, as is that to Aldo Rossi.

In essence, this building can be seen as a palimpsest of the conversations around the subject of Post-Modernism, and the reaction against Late-Modernism. A major ingredient has been the reassessment and use of history to inform and enrich the language. Other references are included and range from Ledoux to Alexander Pope, William Kent and the English landscape tradition.

In practice, the building is likely to become a very important milestone in establishing a tradition of civic and public buildings, possessing an accessible and figurative vocabulary. The Portland and Humana buildings by Michael Graves are others in this category, which will be referred to by those working in the tradition. Their lessons will be augmented and, in the process, changed, adapted and improved.

Massimo Scolari: The Ark

Displayed at the 1986 Milan Triennale, this project continues Scolari's search for an architecture of authenticity. Titled *The Ark*, it is symbolically posited in time after the expulsion from the Garden of Eden, but before the coming cataclysm of the Flood, which will engulf us all, except, of course, those who have been able to find refuge within the primitive and life-saving forms of the Ark. Like all of Scolari's work, it has the power to conjure up deep-seated memories and archetypal images. Here, Scolari, playing two architypes off against each other – the house and the boat – is able to evoke an unease and disequilibrium, which is resolved only by the imposition of the architectural solution. By challenging, decomposing and reversing many of our conventional assumptions about architecture, Scolari is able to remind us of the essential constants of architecture that we are in danger of losing sight of in our pursuit of the mere contingent.

Leon Krier: Atlantis Project, Tenerife

Many of the most potent images and ideas in architecture remain unbuilt. Indeed, their influence is often dependent precisely on this factor – one thinks of Pugin's *Revival of Christian Architecture* and William Morris's *News from Nowhere*. These potent images are often ideals, bound by rules, which we are by definition free to break, if required.

Krier's Tenerife is just such an ideal, but one that will eventually be realised in practice. The pre-industrial Mediterranean imagery suddenly becomes a reality in the post-industrial society and this playground of the rich today may become the commonplace for the many tomorrow, holding out more potential for the urbanist than the earlier ideal of the garden suburb.

Jeremy Dixon: Royal Opera House Extension, London

Irrespective of the political issues surrounding this enterprise – issues that extend well-beyond architecture and concern at the way the Arts should be funded in this country – one cannot but

be impressed by the skill and tenacity in developing and interpreting the brief here. This has involved a very careful historical analysis of the Covent Garden area and its development over the centuries. It is entirely appropriate that the site which witnessed our first steps in classical place-making, through the architecture of Inigo Jones, should now be witnessing our very latest attempts at continuing that tradition.

The classical tradition demands that the mere utilitarian be transcended by taking on something of the transcendental. It is obvious that Jeremy Dixon and his clients understand this. Another aspect is that classicism is a set of values and not a hard and fast set of rules. Change is required and indeed essential in keeping those values alive and it is heartening to see that time is being allowed to evolve, develop and refine the many aspects of this important scheme.

Jean Nouvel: Arab Cultural Centre, Paris

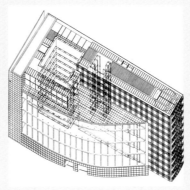

This building is one of Mitterand's grand projects and also a major exercise in diplomacy. Acknowledging and paying respect to Arab culture, it remains resolutely French. Its main feature, used to considerable effect, is the patterned and decorated glazing, which provides richness and allows the curtain wall to extend in reference beyond its usual hermetic and tautologous self. The road alignment is used to good effect by allowing an elliptical plan form to mitigate what would otherwise be a large and conventional office block.

Aldo Rossi: Casa Aurora, Turin

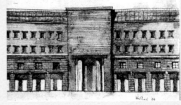

This is a building with a definite urban presence, which reasserts many of those structuring elements by which we read and recognise the city. What at first glance may be taken as banal is subtly redeemed by the controlling idea into an affirmation of the positive. A poetry of the ordinary that is made eloquent by being deliberately contained and restricted within a limited vocabulary, but a vocabulary with a rich and long etymology which we subconsciously read into the forms. However, stripped of this and the accompanying Italian sun, certain elements, for example, the portico/porch at the back of the pavement, may not travel well north of the Alps.

Gae Aulenti: Musée d'Orsay, Paris

The Gare d'Orsay was designed for specific use as a railway terminus. Paris's new museum for 19th-century art would seem to be a model of how such a building can be converted to another use, complementing but not cowed by the original.

Post-Modern forms and free-style classical imagery are combined to produce a modern-day Valhalla. Plain, battered stone walls form a backdrop to the objects and stand in contrast to the massive cast-iron vaults of the original building. Considerable play is made of the changes of level to emphasise the route and enhance in particular the display of sculpture.

Hiroshi Hara: Yamato International, Tokyo

This multi-levelled industrial complex was a deliberate attempt at urban colonisation on a new artificial area outside the Bay of Tokyo. Various scales

are used: the first three floors, used for storage, and abutting an elevated highway, have an engineering scale; the remaining five floors are at a smaller and more recognisably intimate scale.

Seen in the European context, this scheme would be dismissed out of hand for being a megastructure. In the context of Japan, with differing social and cultural constraints, the megastructure may be a valid solution, and should not deter us from acknowledging many of its organisational and architectural qualities.

James Stirling: Science Centre, West Berlin

From the time when this design was first published, it possessed the power to disturb and to console. One's immediate reaction is alarm at the wilful clash of forms on plan, which evoke almost a sense of discomfort, until one finds consolation in the memories of Lou Kahn's Domican Sisters Convent at Media, Pennsylvania, or even in the recollections of Camillo Sitte. We await, with interest, to see if Stirling has been able to evolve a recharged vocabulary in order to clothe the plans with the appropriate urban dress. This is one of the most difficult challenges in civic design today. From the information so far released, the answer would appear to be a definite 'yes'.

Duany and Plater-Zyberk: Vilanova House, Florida

This small house in Florida makes obvious reference to the Erectheion, and to Classical Greece, which appears appropriate and unstrained. The climate, after all, is not too dissimilar and would permit circulation to occur outside.

The massing is arranged to provide a series of controlled views and vistas, as one moves in and around the building and ascends and descends the various levels. The architecture is given an added power by the restraint with which applied decoration is used.

Ralph Lerner: Indira Gandhi National Centre for the Arts, New Delhi

Ralph Lerner's winning entry for the Indira Gandhi National Centre was considered one of the major projects of the year, and deserving recipient of an award. Eclectic in style, making obvious references to the work of Michael Graves and other Post-Modernists, the totality was one of calm distinction. Organised around a series of five courtyards, the forms and their massing gracefully complement and reflect the spaces they enclose. If these can be translated satisfactorily in detail, the Centre will make a very worthy neighbour to Lutyens.

Here is proof that Post-Modernism would appear capable of delivering what Modernism was singularly unable to do: *viz*, to provide a convincing repertoire of forms together with their details, by which civic and institutional ideals can be expressed, celebrated and recorded.

Hans Hollein: Museum of Modern Art, Frankfurt

Hollein has shown that he is master of the episodic and the creator of drama-

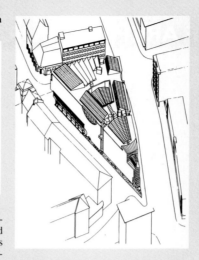

tic set-piece spaces, even if they might not always jell into a convincing architectural totality. Here at Frankfurt, the sophisticated volumetric play of Monchengladbach is continued and the interior architectural space becomes more than ever one of the major exhibits on display. Externally, the elevational elements are dissimulated, with deliberate changes in scale and semantic coding, which we recognise from his very earliest works in Vienna. We can be confident that Hollein will bring to the detailing a typical Viennese precision and elegance.

Gaenz & Rolfes: Hospital, West Berlin

This is a beautifully controlled building, both in plan and elevation; particularly skilful has been the way the architects have broken the accommodation down into manageable parts to form additional external and internal spaces. Equally masterly has been the treatment of the elevations, which complement the plans and reflect a calm reassurance throughout all its parts. This has been achieved by careful use of scale and a subtle application of a limited range of forms and window openings. The clinical has been eschewed, in preference to a more familiar repertoire, without resorting to either the archaic or the arch.

John Blatteau: Interiors/US Department of State, Washington

This is an examplary work of interior architecture, demonstrating that neither invention nor wit need be sacrificed by working within the constraints of an existing building. On the contrary, a freedom can be found with-

in those very limitations, provided the architect is prepared to elevate the needs of the building above his own.

Venturi, Rauch, Scott Brown: National Gallery Extension, London

It is a testimony to enlightened patronage that one of our major civic commissions should go to the person who has done more than any other to change the way that architects think about their work. The influence of Robert Venturi's writing has often obscured the quality of many of his plans and actual work. Now that the commission is secured and approval assured, we can only await with interest the way in which those aspects still to be decided will be dealt with and resolved. It may be that we required an anglophile American, who has been thinking long and hard about English classicism, our Victorian heritage and the lessons of Lutyens to show us how we may learn from our remarkable tradition without recourse to nostalgia or sentiment.

ROUNDUP

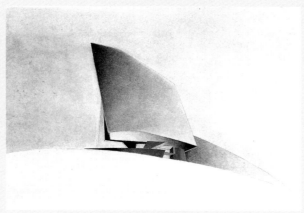

ZAHA HADID, OFFICE BUILDING FOR THE KU'DAMM, BERLIN

DECONSTRUCTION
in Architecture and Urbanism
Architectural Design Vol 58 3/4-1988

If there really is a 'Neo-Modern' architecture, as many architects and critics would wish, then it must rest on a new theory
and practice of Modernism. The only such development to have
emerged in the last twenty years – known as Deconstruction or
Post-Structuralism – takes Modernist elitism and abstraction to
an extreme and exaggerates already known motifs.

This provocative issue of *Architectural Design* is timed to
coincide with Philip Johnson's Deconstructivist architecture
exhibition at the MOMA in New York, as well as the Decon-
structivism Symposium at the Tate Gallery in London. It includes a seminal essay by Charles Jencks and articles and projects
by Bernard Tschumi, Zaha Hadid, Rem Koolhaas, and an
extended interview with Peter Eisenman.

THE NEW MODERNISM
and Deconstructive Tendencies in Art
Art & Design Vol 4 3/4-1988

Contemporary trends in art reveal a creative and questioning
force challenging the basis of accepted aesthetic style, structure
and value. An essential tendency influencing this trend is Deconstruction. Jacques Derrida's philosophical critique of painting
has been a major influence on criticism and consequently painting and sculpture and this issue contains a selection of Derrida's
writings on painting chosen by the translator of his *Truth in
Painting*, Geoff Bennington. The full variety and nature of
Deconstruction in current art is explored. John Griffiths surveys
Deconstructive art, relating it to several philosophical ideologies.
Marco Livingstone assesses the latest work of Mark Lancaster,
while Fred Orton examines the work of Jasper Johns in the light
of its pioneering use of text and image.

Individual issues £7.95/US$14.95 + £1.00/US$3.00 p&p

✂ -

SUBSCRIPTION FORM

☐ I wish to subscribe to **Architectural Design** at the full rate
☐ I wish to subscribe to **AD** at the student rate

☐ I wish to subscribe to **Art & Design** at the full rate
☐ I wish to subscribe to **A&D** at the student rate

☐ I wish to subscribe to **AD** and **A&D** at the full rate
☐ I wish to subscribe to **AD** and **A&D** at the student rate

☐ Starting date: Issue No.................................Year ....
☐ **Please send the individual issues marked.** Value £/US$ ....

☐ **Payment enclosed by Cheque/ P.O./ Draft.** Value £ / US$ ....
☐ **Please charge** £..**to my credit card**

Expiry date:..

Account No:

☐ American Express   ☐ Access/ Mastercharge/ Eurocard
☐ Diners Club   ☐ Barclaycard/ Visa

SUBSCRIPTION RATES

	UK	EUROPE	OVERSEAS
ARCHITECTURAL DESIGN			
Full rate	£45.00	£55.00	US$99.50
Student rate	£39.50	£49.50	US$89.50
ART & DESIGN			
Full rate	£35.00	£39.50	US$75.00
Student rate	£29.00	£35.00	US$65.00
ARCHITECTURAL DESIGN AND ART & DESIGN			
Full combined rate	£65.00	£75.00	US$135.00
Student combined rate	£59.50	£69.50	US$120.00

Signature..
Name..
Address..
....
....

Please send this form with your payment/ credit card authority direct to:

ACADEMY GROUP LTD 7/8 HOLLAND ST, LONDON W8 4NA ✆ 01-402-2141

VISIT THE BOOK FAIR FOR BUSINESS

INTERNATIONAL GATHERING

With the large number of overseas exhibitiors and visitors, the 1988 Fair will be the perfect sales and rights platform for the WORLD BOOK PUBLISHING INDUSTRY

MORE EXHIBITORS

With more exhibitors than ever before, the 1988 London International Book Fair will keep you in touch with the latest developments across every aspect of the book publishing industry.

EVENTS

A combination of conferences, promotions, business and social functions will run throughout the duration of the Fair.

OLYMPIA 2

London's premiere exhibition centre Olympia 2 is easily accessible whether you are travelling by road, rail or air. The facilities provided for visitors at Olympia 2 are excellent, including 3 restaurants, meeting points and lounge areas.

HOTLINE ☎ Katy James/Kari Olsen 01-940 6065

TICKETS JUST £3 IF YOU PRE-REGISTER

NAME _____

JOB TITLE _____

COMPANY _____

ADDRESS _____

_____

POSTCODE _____ COUNTRY _____

Please send me a visitor information pack and details of discounted

registration. Signature _____

Return to: **Katy James**
London International Book Fair 1988
Oriel House, 26 The Quadrant
Richmond, Surrey TW9 1DL
England

Organised by Industrial and Trade Fairs, a member of the Reed Exhibition Companies Limited. Oriel House, 26 The Quadrant, Richmond-upon-Thames, Surrey TW9 1DL ENGLAND. Telex: 929184 CREXCO G, Facsimile: 01-940 2171, Telephone No. 01- 940 6065

PATERNOSTER SQUARE
A Discussion between Leon Krier and Charles Jencks

ROGERS. VIEW FROM PUBLIC SPACE

The decision to redevelop the area to the north of St Paul's has offered a rare chance to amend a Modernist mistake. *Architectural Design* invited Charles Jencks and Leon Krier to its offices to discuss the competition entries in relation to urban planning concepts behind the brief. The brief recognised the sensitivity of the site and specifically stated that the competition was 'to select a Masterplanner, not a scheme, and for competitors to submit conceptual ideas, not designs.'

CJ Quite apart from our views we have to decide what kind of historical or critical justice is going to be done to the schemes, which obviously you're out of sympathy with, sometimes entirely, but I'm willing to consider at least tolerable. All the plans have to be explained positively before they're criticised.

LK One could start with the question of urban space. Some of the schemes consider this just like a huge factory and lay on a grid purely from a production and rent pattern that has nothing to do with the town. The brief asks for 100,000m² of office space and between 9,300 and 14,000m² of commercial retail space. This gives a density over the site of 6·5:1, which is more than the City in principle allows. On top of that, any town planning discipline which respects itself should subtract from the land to start with, allowing, on such a large site, at least 35 to 40 per cent for public space. If we do that we are left with about 11,000m² of buildable site instead of 17,000m². That is what should be done, but because of collusion between developers, the City and the planning authorities, they are going against the law which establishes the densities. 5·11:1 is quite high enough, but while it can be done if calculated over buildable site, if calculated as a raw density it becomes impossible and forces architects into things they shouldn't be doing. You can get the *existing* density with the pre-War plan by making buildings of five floors including gardens, courtyards, streets and squares.

CJ I notice that Richard Rogers assumes a plot ratio of 6·5:1.

LK Well, he has in fact more because he adds to the given brief underground accommodation of 17,000m².

CJ I noticed, however, that roughly half of the entries came in at under 5:1, and what's more they admitted it and said you couldn't get any higher, so I would be wary of accusing them of being in collusion with the City and developers. Both Rogers

and Maccormac produced drawings to show what would happen if they developed to a maximum and then they cut into that. Now it's naive to think of knocking down a 1964 set of buildings and not think that you'll have to pay for it. And the only thing that will is, one, Big Bang large offices, and, two, having St Paul's Cathedral, ie, large offices and a prestige location. These are the rules of the game in a modern, commercial, consumer society and you cannot just blame architects for this – the greater fault lies with the developers – and one cannot just change the rules of the game as you want to do.

LK The argument of profit is not so important. If you could build the same amount of use with a much higher prestige, not just offices, but residences would be economically viable.

CJ So you want to turn this into apartments for the very rich – and some kind of luxury boutique office buildings, which is what Isozaki wanted in addition to large-span offices? Instead of the government subsidising a mixture of uses and classes you want to turn it into an upper-class area?

LK I am not necessarily against that. It is important that the town again becomes inhabited as a place of work and residence, who can afford it is not for us to decide. The problem for the architect is to deliver a structure which allows these things to happen elegantly and pleasantly.

CJ Yes, it's best that the site be developed from the point of mixed use, but the argument that doesn't see the responsibility of the architect knowing the price of those luxury apartments or its social mix would be just as culpable, just as cynical as caving in to property developers.

This debate *is* open and continuing. It's a pseudo-conspiracy that said the developers were going to build without consulting the public. Why do you think they consulted Prince Charles?

VII

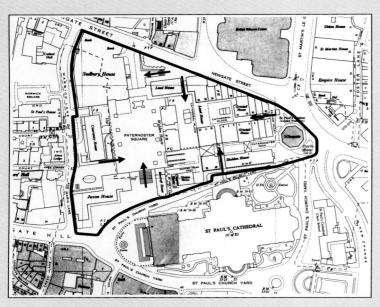 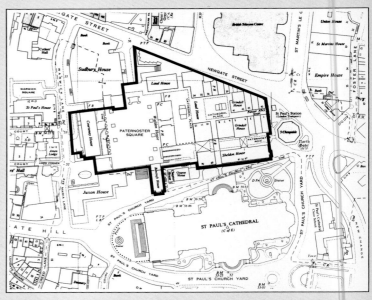

L TO R: MASTERPLAN SITE; AREA CURRENTLY UNDER CONTROL OF PCL

The Prince has explained the sort of process he wants to see surrounding St Paul's – brick buildings of a kind that were built in Wren's time, and a low density – without describing their use, beyond outlining a scheme which will increase the amount of tourists from three to seven or eight million. Now, he says it makes hard-headed economic commercial sense to in fact turn this area into some kind of giant industrial tourism – he doesn't use those words, he doesn't see those implications, but to service seven or eight million people and pay for the price of three-storey brick Wren-like tourist offices or millionaire apartments is socially impossible. The reality is that hard-headed business assumes there are going to be so many prestige offices with large-span floors in there and in fact that kind of typology does not fit completely into three-storey brick – and even if it did, is the image of three-storey brick housing the right one for Big Bang multi-nationals?

LK Making big offices is considered to be realism. I think it's lunatic, the will of a very small minority. The problem is to stop this totally mad speculation on urban land which destroys cities.

CJ These are big multi-national corporations each trying to build, as the Prince said about Manhattan, a 'bigger slice of the tower' close to St Paul's. This is prestige power fighting each other, this is what the image of Isozaki's is.

LK But this is fantasy and they know it is no longer acceptable. In all the briefs, including the brief given to the architects, there was a lot of talk of history and that shows they know it is not at all the right thing to put there. Otherwise they wouldn't talk so much about context, they would just say 'here is an office factory and we are going to build a bloody factory there.'

CJ This expression of office-blocks as monuments to corporations is as real today as the church steeple was in the 17th century. This would never have come to a head if the developers and the pressure for Big Bang offices were not there. Why didn't John Simpson and the Prince and you start out by saying: 'Hey, north of St Paul's was bombed during the war and we hate the Holford scheme, let's tear it down'? Why? Because you don't think realistically, you react to what you consider the bad movements of capital and power, to something which has preceded you. The developers stepped in and they are tearing down something that was finished in 1964, which is incredible, historically – we have never had such a gigantic piece of Modernism torn down. For the Prince to presume he can go back to the 17th-

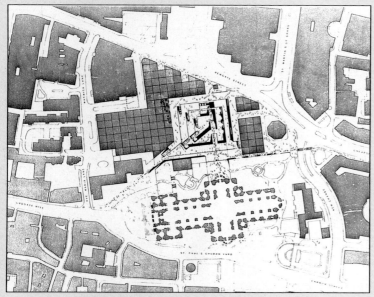 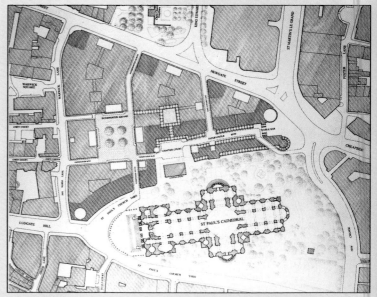

GROUND PLANS. *L TO R:* ROGERS, SOM

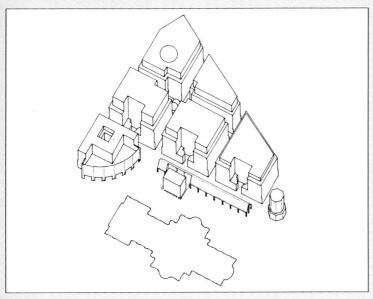 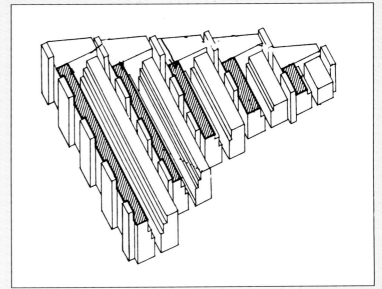

AXONOMETRIC PLANS. *L TO R:* STIRLING, FOSTER

century city of spires dominating three- to four-storey brick buildings is a regression in economic and social terms. We don't live in a Christian society dominated by the church, we live in a mercantile culture.

LK Everybody sane agrees St Paul's should continue to dominate the skyline.

CJ Absolutely, but all of these peole *have* agreed with that. These architects have *all* produced a medievalesque plan in Big Bang terms. For me Rogers has produced a medieval High-Tech, whilst Norman Foster produces something like ten Burlington Arcades all in a row, all in a very tightly networked field of alleyways. All of these schemes are Post-Modernist Classical plans in a general typological sense, no one has seen slabs in a park. I would argue that there has been a shift: there is a new typology at work here.

LK That is because there is such a density requested they cannot do anything but dense urban blocks. A good historical, traditional town plan needs 30 to 40 per cent of public space. Rogers did one diagram which says 80 per cent usage, but there the alleys are so narrow, they are not alleys. If you have narrow alleys which are pleasant, you cannot build over a certain height

without them becoming nightmares. The reaction in Victorian times was to make very large streets because that's the only way to get proper light at the ground floor. Now medieval town plans were so narrow because they were only one or two storeys high. I'm not saying that people consciously do wrong but there is so much negligence that there is no political choice. Decisions taken in the City or elsewhere on density are not informed; if you could show what they would get at different densities then they could consciously choose.

CJ Shall we discuss some plans. Rogers you can see rejecting as a catastrophy Le Corbusier's Saint-Die Modernist plan and wanting to go to a positive-negative figural density which is like a traditional one. On his very important urban context page, you see him comparing the Parma ground plan with Saint-Die, and Le Corbusier open-plan figural buildings with the existing figural buildings seen as objects in a park, in an attempt to get back to medieval small streets, alleyways, little squares, a big piazza or atrium in front of the north transept and a proper carved out view of the west front. You *cannot* deny that Rogers has seen the positive virtue.

LK With that kind of width you just cannot do eight-storey

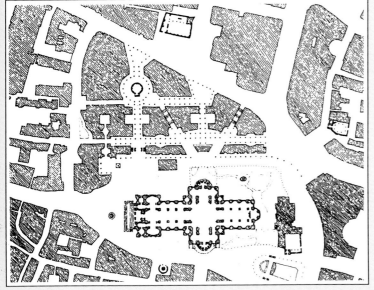 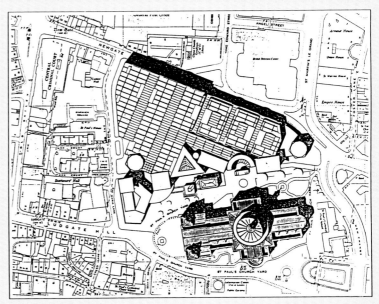

GROUND PLANS. *L TO R:* MACCORMAC, ISOZAKI

IX

MACCORMAC, *L TO R:* EAST-WEST, NORTH-SOUTH AND RADIAL STREETS

high buildings, it's an absurdity.

CJ No, because a lot of these things go underground. Let's look at the relative height against the existing Chapter House.

LK It was the height of the urban fabric around St Paul's, the height of the first entablature, which created the effect of St Paul's standing there like a huge altar on which sits a tabernacle.

CJ I don't think that is quite a true interpretation. I'm going to argue that Wren didn't want a two-storey elevation because his first plan and his third plan were in favour of a grand order. For his third scheme he produced the giant order which made an incredible set piece of the west front – a temple, two towers with lanterns and the centrepiece of the dome – but he couldn't do it, because he found out that Portland stone was not strong enough to hold the portico as it came away from the building. I think Wren wanted it to be seen in a great Baroque set-piece view, only he couldn't physically build it, so he had to go to a French two-storey solution that's led Gavin Stamp and others to asume that he actually wanted tantalising glimpses of St Paul's. In Hawksmoor's important 1710-11 plan, there is a three-quarter round Piazza with colonnade, a Corinthian Order going round the whole wedge shape and then a baptistry from which one can imagine one would achieve this incredible set-piece.

LK But this square is much narrower, much more enclosed than anybody here is doing and the height . . .

CJ Is five storeys.

LK Well, it's not higher than the present entablature.

CJ Anyway, his plan has certain assumptions that have been talked about by everyone – small alleyways, small streets coming in – *plus* one grand vista coming in slightly off-axis, one grand Piazza and the implication of two lesser ones.

LK So you're saying it's not a large building floating in a square, but three squares, of which the front one is more important than the sides and the sides are not straight, but are just the streets linking these squares. That's a very important perception which none of the competitors understood.

CJ That's right. The interesting thing about the Cathedral is that it's a compromise between a longitudinal Gothic plan and a Baroque and Renaissance central plan and it makes a virtue out of that compromise. The 1710-11 plan is also a compromise between a medieval small street arcaded view, let's call it the 'Little England' view with only glimpses, and the large Baroque view. The plan has a contradiction and complexity built into it

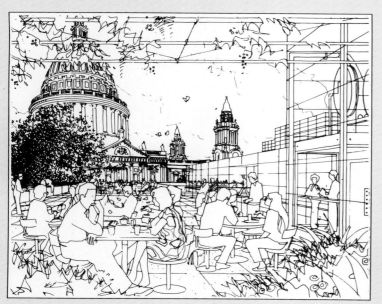

RELATIONSHIP WITH CATHEDRAL, *L TO R:* FOSTER, SOM

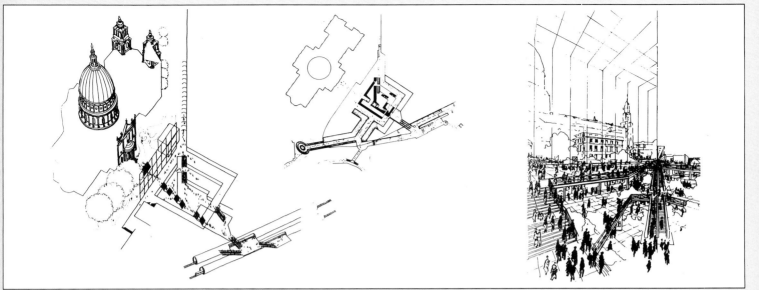

ROGERS, ATRIUM CONNECTING UNDERGROUND TO CATHEDRAL

between two opposite, conflicting views of how to handle it – and it makes a virtue of it. Arup's won partly because they have the same mixture. If you look at plans of the past, the view of the north transept has always been conceived as a street. There is a tradition of approaching the Cathedral from the north and south which makes a focus of the apsidal or exedra-like projection taken from Pietra da Cortona's Santa Maria della Pace. The winning scheme, a combination of Arup's and Rogers, quite rightly makes a pedestrianised Piazza in front of that.

LK But bigger than the one foreseen by Hawksmoor.

CJ But that's because of the way the road cuts through the site. The Arup scheme acknowledges the road up Ludgate Hill, cutting through the potential Piazza, and so rotates the Piazza at right angles to the street to give a well-scaled view of the dome.

LK But Arup's make the 19th-century mistake of freeing the monument from all the little things around it.

CJ I agree none of the designs really made enough of the contrast between tight space and figural voids. The most extreme example is in the Maccormac scheme. They said explicitly you must enclose it with dense urban tissue, you must have glimpses, yet it's as if they didn't read their own brief.

LK The problem in big architectural competitions is that they involve urban issues which very few architects are used to dealing with. They are not trained urbanists and they consider the site as one building, one system, one grid.

CJ Well that's why I was not alone in favouring having three or four architects working on this according to a Masterplan. Maccormac gives an analysis of the necessity for a tight contextual fabric to surround an open monument, but then produces a leaky, eroded plan – which is true also of Stirling to a degree, and certainly true of Isozaki and Foster. Foster's historical analysis is quite sophisticated and even picks up, which no one else did, the shift in the grid. He then wants to reinforce the shift so he puts in this dense fabric of High-Tech and thin arcades focusing and dramatising it, but again the problem is the serrated edge and leaking spaces. They see the problem and yet none of them can really deal with it.

Let me mention an interesting aspect of both Foster and Rogers. They both talk about the 'fifth elevation' – the roofs. Now being on the roof can be incredibly exciting. From it, at cornice height, you would really see what you claim you could in the Middle Ages. Foster, Rogers, Arup's all had fantastic roof

RELATIONSHIP WITH CATHEDRAL, *L TO R:* ISOZAKI, STIRLING

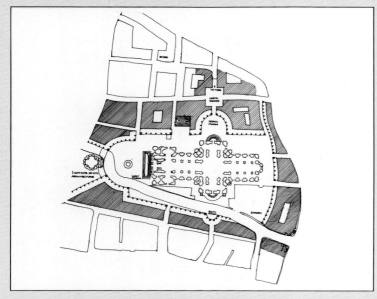 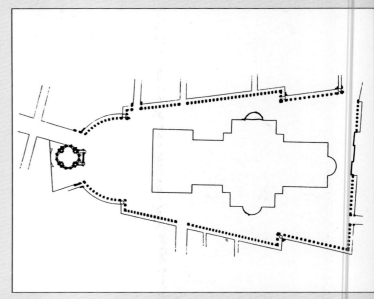

L TO R: JENCKS, PLAN COMBINING SEVERAL SCHEMES AND EMBEDDING CATHEDRAL; HAWKSMOOR PLAN, 1710-11

schemes.

What about the SOM plan, which in a way comes closest to the Simpson plan and your concerns? As I would suggest ought to be done, they continue the King Edward Street vista into a lane that focuses on the north front, but then they stick a hotel across it and block the view.

LK That's not necessarily so tragic because the most important thing here is a view of the mass.

CJ Well it seems a shame not to at least allow people to go through the hotel at ground level, so when you come out you see it again. Also, as in all the schemes, the Chapter House floats like an untouchable.

LK The way the streets are mapped there may be correct but is not I think very interesting.

CJ In this scheme you get a good idea of how a certain percentage of their blocks are filled in by Big Bang offices, and if ever there's a firm that's hyper super-realistic about the requirements it is SOM. I would call this an Edwardian typology, rather than 17th century, it's much heavier and coarser in grain.

LK Most of the plans have six or seven blocks. The pre-War plan had about 19, bissected by many narrow alleyways so they were very fine grain.

CJ The Rogers scheme has something not unlike that.

LK The Rogers plan is mechanical, it lays a grid over the whole site, SOM's could be conceived as different buildings.

CJ I'm not sure it's true, that's hardly mechanical.

LK It's on a constructive grid.

CJ It's an articulated grid though, not a rigid mechanical one. He varies the size of the blocks. It's true the streets don't curve, but there's more grain and texture in the Rogers plan than in the SOM plan, because he provides large streets and smaller alleys. There's a great virtue in his scheme: you arrive by tube into this little Piazza, look up the escalators into another enclosed atrium and another one and then you see the dome through glass. Now in one direction it's fantastic, but looking back it's not so fantastic. So the whole rub is very much in how you treat that glass wall and I criticised this heavily, although I thought, conceptually, it was a brilliant idea. You finally connect up in a way that is very 20th-century, that is, we do travel by tube and one of the great things which ought to exist in our culture is to arrive at a tube stop and have a sense of arrival.

LK It's an atrium as if it were Grand Central.

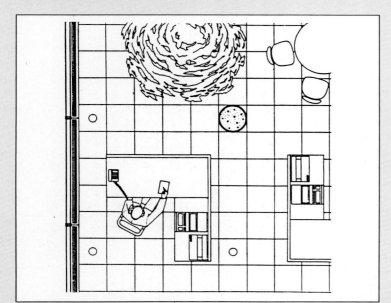 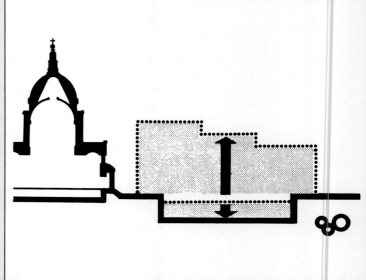

L TO R: ISOZAKI, OFFICE DESIGN; ROGERS, HEIGHT ANALYSIS

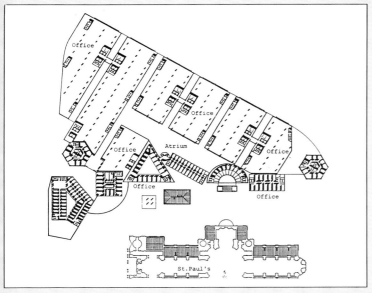 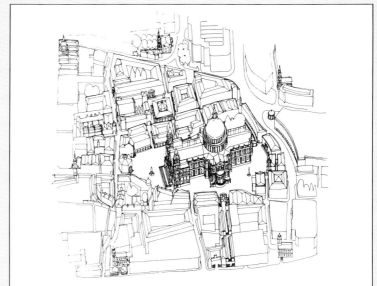

L TO R: ISOZAKI, TYPICAL OFFICE FLOOR; SIMPSON, GROUND PLAN

CJ You took the words out of my mouth, as I said to him at the time, this is a great idea, but there are so many escalators, so many steps, so many people moving, there's no place to relax and enjoy it.

LK The problem is they are making the big space where it ought not to be and are competing with the proper square in front of the Cathedral.

CJ It doesn't need to be half as big as this, it's just a possible connection that ought to be celebrated. We've taken one point from one person's scheme because it happened to fit with the winning scheme. Four other architects are going to be designing aspects of Arup's scheme. Rogers should design the atrium because he thought of it, it's his invention – it would be a kind of stealing if you were to combine the best ideas of all of them and give them to Arup's.

Let's discuss the Simpson plan. I agree it has some very nice assumptions from your brief, the basic one of which is a mixed use and a less oppressive, less monofunctional building typology, it's changed the rules of the game. Having said that, I still don't feel it makes a proper piazza out of the west front.

LK I agree that is the weak part of the scheme but the important thing is he fills up the gap.

CJ Which is very positive but he should have pulled it in tighter. I feel, to offer my own solution, that one should come much closer to the back of the Cathedral and really build very tight up against it, just cutting out a north, south and west approach, but with the road through to get in all of those horrible tourist bus stops.

LK The important thing is to have tension. Building closer to the church would give more space to build on and tension to the space at front and side. The winning plan suffers exactly all the weaknesses of the others: it's far too far away from the Cathedral and has a monumental facade which is obstructive and competes too much with St Paul's.

CJ You must wait. The Arup solution has not yet been finalised and has some good points: it solves the problem of the piazzetta, acknowledges traffic flow allowing traffic to go to one side and opens a northern piazzetta focusing on the transept. The debate is in danger of becoming a stalemate – I've tried in my scheme to pull several of the best ideas together in order to push the discussion on to the next step.

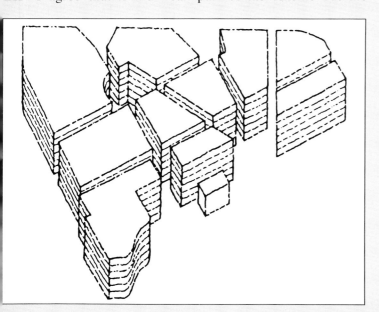 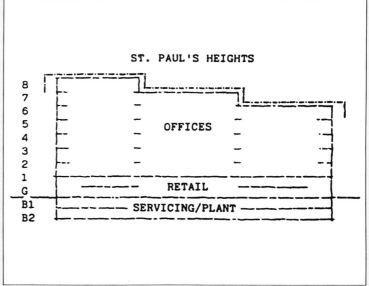

MACCORMAC, *L TO R:* BUILDING ENVELOPES; USAGE LEVELS

ROUNDUP

**Eileen Gray: Architect/Designer:
A Biography**
Peter Adam
Abrams, New York, Thames &
Hudson, London 1987
400 pages, b&w and col ills. Cloth

**Les Villas D'Artistes A Paris:
de Louis Süe à Le Corbusier**
*Jean-Claude Delorme, photographs by
Stephane Couturier*
Les Editions de Paris, Paris, 1987
256 pages, b&w and col ills. Paper NP

Two recent books focus on the architectural and design avant-garde in Paris in the first half of this century, when Paris was not only the home of the Cubists and Le Corbusier, but the centre of intellectual ferment – the Paris of Gide, Cocteau, Colette and Gertrude Stein.

Eileen Gray, architect and designer, flew with Chéron and had a 'close friendship' with the *chanteuse* Damia. She built only three houses, (although she designed several more) – *E1027*, the house in Cap Martin for Badovici; the *Tempe à Pailla*, her own house at Castellar; and *Lou Perou*, the house she built near St Tropez after the Second World War – but she was responsible for the creation of some of the most opulent and sophisticated lacquer furniture of the pre-First World War years and then of furniture that epitomised the ideals of the 20s, of the Bauhaus and De Stijl. Her adjustable tubular steel furniture and geometric carpets were famous at that time, but although she only died in 1976, she was then largely forgotten until she was rediscovered in the 1970s and seen as an important innovator. An independent and original figure, her designs appeal to the trends of today (several of them, notably the Bibendum and Non-Conformist chairs and various adjustable chrome tables, are now manufactured by Aram Designs) and can be valued for their originality and avant-garde appeal.

The book is both a biography and study of her designs. Starting with her childhood in Ireland and London, interspersed by visits abroad to visit her artist father who had left the family when Eleanor was a child; the author stresses the desire for independence that led her in 1901 not into marriage but to study at the Slade. She was taught by Steer, Tonks and Brown and her friends included Gerald Kelly and Wyndham Lewis, both of whom she later knew in Paris. She became interested in furniture when she was at the Slade and made frequent visits to the V&A. She then moved to Paris, and with two friends studied at the Academie Julien, but growing bored with painting, gradually began to design furniture. Her early pieces were influenced by Art Nouveau – the simple lines of the Arts and Crafts, Mackintosh and Vienna styles rather than the more florid highly decorated Franco-

Belgian style. She had enormous enthusiasm for trying out new materials and paid great attention to detail, learning how to perfect the technique of lacquer making and perservering until she achieved a blue colour everyone had said was impossible. Her first exhibition at the *Salon des Artistes Décoratifs* in 1913 led to commissions for tables and an extravagant tasselled lacquer sofa for wealthy couturier and collector Jacques Doucet and later to the design of a complete apartment for Madame Mathieu-Lévy, with stark, sculptural, Cubist-influenced, black lacquer brick-screen hallway and opulent salon. Disillusioned with producing only a few luxury items – lacquer was of necessity very slow and expensive to produce – she opened a shop to try and reach a wider public. She became interested in new industrial techniques and designing pieces that could be possible prototypes for mass production, using chromed tubular steel elements, zinc, aluminium, screens from industrial grids, as well as exotic woods. Her 'Monte Carlo' room at the 1923 *Salon* attracted the attention of Mallet-Stevens and of the Dutch De Stijl group: Jan Wils wrote the introduction to a special issue in 1924 of the Dutch magazine, *Wendingen*, featuring her work.

It was her friendship with the young architect and editor of *L'Architecture Vivante*, Jean Badovici, that encouraged her growing interest in architecture and familiarity with the new

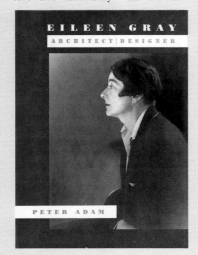

movements and theories of the time. Through him she became acquainted with, amongst others, Le Corbusier. Eileen was already interested through her interior design in problems of space. Architecture allowed her to extend this preoccupation to consider total space, exterior as well as interior, and to give her as architect as well as designer, total command over the environment created. *E1027* uses most of Le Corbusier's five principles – pilotis, terraces, modern materials, purist forms – together with her own touches, ingenious fitted furniture, clever win-

dow arrangements, without ever losing touch of the human element.

Perhaps it was as a woman, Slade-trained as an artist, but self-trained as an architect and thus outside the predominantly male architectural and design establishment that makes for her individuality. Le Corbusier admired her architecture and included her design for a *Centre des Vacances* – a social

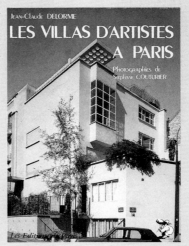

complex accommodating new ideas of holidays for the masses, with facilities such as restaurants, cinemas and play areas by the sea – in his *Pavillon des Temps Nouveaux* at the *International Exposition* in Paris in 1937. But as a loner, not part of any particular group but always on the fringes, she has been left out of many books. Her self-training meant she was less rule-bound than many of the establishment architects, but also that she lacked many of their contacts: most of her projects remained unbuilt and her furniture only achieved mass production after her death.

Peter Adam attempts to show how Eileen Gray's designs were both a part of the Modern Movement and distinctively her own. The book is well written and readable and well illustrated with black and white (many of them her own) and colour photographs, plans of her designs and photographs of her and her circle, including the elegant profile portrait by Berenice Abbott, although perhaps there could also have been some comparative photographs of the works of her contemporaries. Peter Adam makes good use of contemporary sources and also his own knowledge of Eileen who he got to know in her old age. As combined biography and thematic study of her fields of design, the chronology is sometimes a little confusing and, also, having created a useful *catalogue raisonné* at the back, the numbers given to her pieces in this could perhaps have been used for the illustrations or for cross-referencing with the text. However on the whole he succeeds well in bringing his subject across and also gives a good back-

ground picture of the Paris milieu of the time. It is a sympathetic portrait of an original, very independent woman, modest but easily hurt by criticism. Adam tends to concentrate quite heavily on Eileen's architecture, which possibly unbalances the book, as in many ways it is here that her role must necessarily remain a relatively minor one. It seems probable that her greatest originality and more lasting influence is in her furniture and interior design, both the Modernist tubular metal furniture and the earlier designs, that she herself later reacted against, but in their black elegance have wide appeal today.

It is ironical that Eileen Gray wished to build social schemes but the only houses she built were for herself or closely associated friends. Similarly, with the exception of the *Unité*, Marseilles, it is his private houses that seem to best exemplify Le Corbusier's ideals, not the grand social schemes he so much desired. *Les Villas d'Artistes à Paris* by Jean-Claude Delorme is in this sense approached from another angle – to a similar result. The author specifically looks at the Modern Movement from the point of view of individual houses and studios in Paris built for artists, designers and collectors, arguing that these are the patrons who will dare to have the most original and exciting works. He points out that Le Corbusier, who is the final figure in this book, built no official buildings in Paris, yet a dozen individual houses and studios have becomes models of architecture. Eileen Gray is not mentioned in this book but she certainly was acquainted with several of those who are.

Les Villas d'Artistes à Paris is lucidly written and well illustrated mainly in black and white. A general introduction is followed by chapters on individual architects, starting with Louis Süe and with the pioneering use of reinforced concrete by Auguste Perret and following through with the various strands of Modernism. Each architect is covered first by a general introduction to his work and then a look in detail at individual projects that still remain in Paris. Some of these are well known, such as Adolf Loos' house for the Dadaist writer Tristan Tzara, others less known, such as Pierre Chareau's unusual 'Maison de verre', Adolphe Thiers' artists' studios and André Lurcat's stunning Purist Maison Guggenbhul, that is shown on the front cover. The majority of the houses are grouped in three main areas of Paris – just south of the Bois de Boulogne, near Montmartre, and near the Parc du Montsouris – (sadly the small-scale map is very poorly reproduced), the book could thus be used both as a history of Modernism, the application of new architectural theories to an existing environment, and as an interesting guide to an often overlooked aspect of Paris.

The Villas of Palladio
Photographs by Philip Trager, Text by Vincent Scully
Little Brown & Co. Boston, 1987
167 pages, b&w ills, Cloth, £29.95

Atmospheric photographs casting evocative images of Palladio's villas in a still, empty, often misty landscape. Empty of people they give the architecture a timeless quality. Many of the views are from afar, seen from slightly decaying gardens or neglected fields, central trees emphasise the symmetry. Other photos focus gently on details – corners, parts of statues, wall decorations, the simple airy spaces of the Villa Pojana. The book is well-designed, without it being obtrusive, varying larger and smaller images, views and close-ups. The photographs are attractively produced in duotone, which gives a softness and subtle range and suitably nostalgic feel.

The short text by Vincent Scully is very American. Whilst he comments interestingly on developments in Palladio's style, from the solidity of the early Villa Godi, through the exuberance of Villa Barbaro, to the stark classical purity of late Villa Emo, the main bias is towards deterministic influence on America, giving a slightly odd, rather anachronistic emphasis for the European reader. Analogies are drawn not only with Jefferson's Neo-Classicism, but also Venturi's Post-Modernism, and even the raised ground floors of Frank Lloyd Wright and the Prairie houses of the American Mid-West.

Restaurant Design
Susan Colgan
The Architectural Press, London, 1987
256 pages, col ills. Cloth, NP

An attractive, amusing and colourful survey of restaurant design in the 80's. the author looks at 95 restaurants (predominently in the United States) considering how the type and image of the food served, the location, space and budget are all factors in the creation of the desired atmosphere. The technical detail in the text may imply that it is ostensibly for architects and designers, but the photographic style makes it as much a book for foodies. Interior design of restaurants is obviously marching hand-in-hand with the aesthetic preoccupations of nouvelle cuisine food. Decoration is back and Pop is still in to judge from most of the restaurants – neon lights, cartoon characters, and bright colours feature alongside columns and arches, where frequently whimsical Post-Modern detail is at its closest to Pop. If one wants restraint one is most likely to find it in ethnic restaurants (trying to break free from old stereotypes) or in the more traditional hotel dining rooms; in theme bars, take-outs and nightspots, a bit like fancy dress, the emphasis is on the busy, on colour and on ornament.

THE ACADEMY FORUM AT THE TATE

B Tschumi

BERNARD TSCHUMI, EXPLODED *FOLIE*, 1984, DETAIL.

INTERNATIONAL SYMPOSIUM ON
DECONSTRUCTION
T H E   N E W   M O D E R N I S M

One-day symposium at the Auditorium, Tate Gallery, Millbank SW1, on Saturday, 26th March, 1988, 9.30 AM to 5.50 PM

Deconstruction is one of the most exciting tendencies in art, architecture and criticism today. Artists have responded strongly to Jacques Derrida's controversial philosophy of deconstruction and more recently a number of architects have explored its implications for their work – most dramatically Bernard Tschumi at the Parc de la Villette in Paris, where Peter Eisenman has also collaborated with Derrida to create 'an architecture of heterogeneity, interruption, non-coincidence'. The symposium will examine current work in architecture and the arts in France, Britain and America. Speakers include Bernard Tschumi, Peter Eisenman, Charles Jencks, Zaha Hadid, Geoff Bennington, and Craig Owens.

The Academy Forum is the result of collaboration between the Tate Gallery and the Academy Group. This collaboration gives access to important financial and editorial resources and ensures the participation of international artists, architects and critics, thereby establishing a high standard of critical debate.

Deconstruction, The New Classicism and *British Art Now* are the themes of the first programme of symposia to be held in the Tate Gallery Auditorium in March, July and October. They will be complemented by lectures, debates and discussions on related subjects at the Tate and elsewhere.

The symposium will be held on Saturday March 26th from 9.30am to 5.50pm. Admission free by ticket only. For further details write to Academy Group Ltd., 42 Leinster Gardens, London, W2 3AN, or The Education Department, Tate Gallery, Millbank, London, SW1P 4RG.

The New Classicism

IN ARCHITECTURE AND URBANISM

MICHAEL GRAVES, ERICKSON ALUMNI CENTER, WEST VIRGINIA UNIVERSITY

TORINO, AR 85

ALDO ROSSI, CASA AURORA, TURIN, DETAIL OF FACADE

The New Classicism
IN ARCHITECTURE AND URBANISM

JOSE-IGNACIO LINAZOSORO, DEGUE UNIVERSITY

THIS ISSUE EXAMINES THE EMERGENCE OF A new classicism in architecture, which is fiercely controversial with its implied rejection and negation of Modernism. *Architectural Design* has consistently explored this movement since the beginning of the decade when, following the strong classicist content of the architectural exhibition at the 1980 Venice Biennale, it invited members of its editorial board and other major critics – including Charles Jencks, Demetri Porphyrios, John Onians, Christian Portzamparc and Quinlan Terry – to debate the issue in a symposium at its offices. It quickly became clear that there are two conflicting views on how classicism applies to contemporary practice: while some want simply to re-establish past values and rules, others argue for a flexible interpretation of the classical tenets in terms appropriate to a post-industrial society.

Out of these divergent stances grew two separate, seminal issues of *Architectural Design*: 'Free-Style Classicism', in which Charles Jencks looked at an architecture of eclecticism, and the violently opposed, polemically entitled, 'Classicism is not a Style' guest-edited by Demetri Porphyrios. This present issue, therefore, whilst by no means the first on the theme, is a particularly important one in that it brings together in the same volume the major opposing viewpoints at a time when classicist consciousness is visibly present not only in drawing but in much executed architecture today. Both the main essays and the example of the projects presented, eloquently sum up the wealth of classicism today.

Front Cover: Aldo Rossi, Marburg Museum, drawing of the interior courtyard. *Back Cover:* Demetri Porphyrios, House in Kensington, painting by Rita Wolff

Photo: Mark Fiennes

QUINLAN TERRY, RICHMOND RIVERSIDE DEVELOPMENT

Editor: Dr Andreas C Papadakis

First published in Great Britain in 1988 by *Architectural Design*
an imprint of the
ACADEMY GROUP LTD, 7 HOLLAND STREET, LONDON W8 4NA

Architectural Design Profile 70 is published as part of *Architectural Design* Volume 58 1/2-1988
Distributed in the United States of America by
St Martin's Press, 175 Fifth Avenue, New York 10010

ISBN: 0-85670-938-7 (UK)
ISBN: 0-312-01906-8 (USA)

Printed in Great Britain by E G Bond Ltd, London

CLIVE ASLET
Classicism for the Year 2000

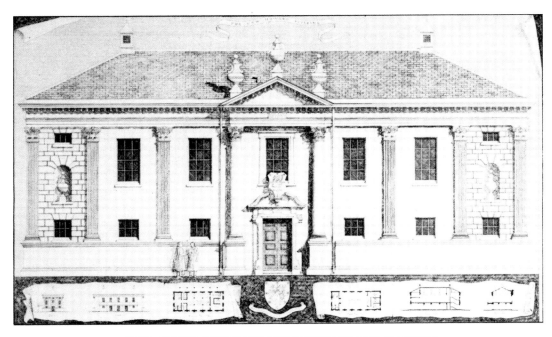

QUINLAN TERRY, HOWARD BUILDING, DOWNING COLLEGE, CAMBRIDGE

The classical revival has suffered from the stigma of its paradoxical association with both popularity and fascism, yet it is undoubtedly making a comeback. Clive Aslet looks at the positive qualities – the permanent cultural values, the rationality and comprehensibility that underlie its populism, the monumentality and presence that have lent its forms to politicisation – and argues that far from being 'fascist', it is the source of hope for a future of 'real' architecture.

I am a Millenialist. I do not mean this in a strictly religious sense, though some would say that a Second Coming could have a greater impact on architecture than even the Prince of Wales' recent pronouncements. But I do believe that by the year 2000 the world will have seen the return of real architecture, and that some pretty fancy footwork will be required from both the quick and the dead if their reputation – perhaps their souls – are to survive.

What is real architecture? It is architecture that ordinary people recognise as being architecture, where buildings are not only beautifully finished and nobly proportioned but articulated, ornamented and expressed. In other words it is classicism. It is an architecture of rules and erudition. But unlike all the forms of Modernism and its descendants it is instinctively recognised and understood by ordinary people, having evolved as part of the common language of civilisation over 3,000 years.

This decade has seen a revival of classicism in Britain. It is on a tiny scale when looked at in comparison to the full total of what is being built, but not on such a tiny scale when the yardstick is media coverage. Most buildings – the vast majority – arouse not a flicker of public interest when they are unveiled (unless they have been part of a conservationist *cause célèbre*). This must be a matter of chagrin to their architects. Yet classical buildings always excite comment. Small exhibitions on modern classical architecture, such as those at the Building Centre in 1984 and 1987, are reviewed with an intensity out of all proportion to their size. It is one indication that this fledgling movement – with only a few buildings to its credit, and most of those, private houses –

is set to become a major phenomenon by the end of the century. The situation is similar to that of Modernism in the late 1920s, with one exception: Modernism had to battle against a hostile public. The new classicism has only (in some cases) to fight reluctant planning officers: public opinion is already overwhelmingly on its side.

There are many reasons why a revival of classicism can be predicted. One is historical. After the Second World War the most desperate need of the country was to build. Partly the damage caused by the Luftwaffe had to be made good, partly utopian visions of a better-housed population seemed urgent and imperative. That these utopian visions did not work out in practice is another story. Here it is enough to remember that the presiding ethic was like that of the supermarket moghul: pile 'em high, build 'em cheap. This great rebuilding of Britain finished in the 1970s. There is now no clamour to build; if anything a shudder of apprehension is felt whenever a building site is seen. Today's need it to make lovely what we have; slowly to replace the eyesores; little by little to upgrade the urban fabric. As a nation we are also gaining the surplus wealth with which to do it.

Another reason is technical. Classicism is a style of repeated elements, but of elements that are often rather complicated to make. Until recently they have defeated anything like mass production, except for the acceptable use of artificial stone. But with the development of more sophisticated technology this position is changing. It is becoming increasingly easy to have large runs of stone mouldings, for example, cut to specification.

Classicism is becoming cheaper.

Yet another reason is financial. The 1970s was the decade of conservation. In the late 1980s it seems that the conservation lobby is in danger of shouting itself hoarse: while there will always be fierce arguments among the professionals about the finer points of restoration – how far historic interiors can be altered, for example – the great battles that captured the public imagination have been fought. It seems unlikely that there will be another Euston Arch. Instead the public is excited by the plurality of styles used by living architects, and will increasingly turn its attention to new architecture, new design. But the legacy of the conservation movement survives in planning. There is scarcely any site in central London, for instance, which does not have historic buildings implications. If it does not involve the demolition of a listed building, it is likely to be in a conservation area or next to a building which is listed. It is not perhaps logical to say that classical buildings are, of themselves, more conservationist than Modern or Post-Modern ones. They are new architecture, not conservation. But undoubtedly they are more likely to conform to an historic context because of their materials and idiom. Developers are noticing this more and more. A classical

inside, not to mention irresistible Greek-inspired furniture.

In Sweden, Stockholm Town Hall – graceful, romantic, witty, and one of the most published buildings of the age – was begun in 1902 but not finished until 20 years later; in the 1920s came a revival of stricter classical forms which recalled the golden age of King Gustavus III in the 18th century. At that time the Swedish court was under the influence of French Neo-Classicism, so the great works of 1920s classicism in Sweden have a strong rationalist element. This led Asplund, the genius of the movement, in the direction of Modernism after 1930. But he returned to a kind of abstract classicism in his last works, and even his Modernist buildings have a relationship to his classicism, albeit a negative one, since in them it almost seems that he was exploring the extent to which it was possible to deny each and every tenet of his earlier style.

Finland is a more rural country, but – leaving aside the early work of Alvar Aalto – it still produced two masterpieces of classicism in utterly contrasting modes. The Parliament Building in the capital Helsinki is hard as steel, though with a redeeming elegance of detail. By contrast the Kapyla Garden Suburb, with its wooden houses decorated with flat wooden

L TO R: CARL PETERSEN, FAABORG MUSEUM, DENMARK; IVAR TENGBOM, CONCERT HALL, STOCKHOLM, 1921-8

Photo: Demetri Porphyrios

design will canter through the planning process in record time, whereas the Modernist equivalent falls at the first hurdle. To the developer, probably financed by borrowed money, delays are expensive. Can he afford *not* to go classical?

To some people classicism still seems about as cranky as health food or homoeopathy. When the history of 20th-century architecture is taken as a whole, however, there is no basis for this prejudice. There has been a rich (if broken) tradition of classical building in many parts of the world, though this has been virtually ignored by the history books. Let us take a quick glance around the world.

In Scandinavia Neo-Classicism had Nationalist overtones and this helped inspire a new classical architecture in the years before and after the First World War. Denmark began it with the Faaborg Museum, a tiny building constructed on a long sliver of land next to a jam factory, which was nevertheless ingeniously planned, handsomely furnished in Empire style, and had a classical entrance which, despite the small scale, recalls Ledoux. Immediately after the War came the Copenhagen Police Headquarters, externally gaunt (in the manner of early 19th-century Danish Neo-Classicism) but with Mannerist touches

pediments and doorcases, is the reverse of severe: it is colourful and charming and elegant and economical – in fact a perfect model for modern speculative builders.

In Britain and her dominions classicism survived as, in part, the appropriate expression of an imperial power. Until the Second World War it was the natural language of all great public buildings, whether the prestige headquarters of professional institutions in London or the civic halls, libraries and law courts of provincial towns. Even London Transport, the model progressive patron, built stations designed on classical principles, with stripped-down classical detailing. Everything changed after the War, of course, but even in the 1950s and 1960s it was possible for some intelligent public buildings to be built in a classical style: witness McMoran and Whitby's work at Nottingham University or Raymond Erith's at Gray's Inn. In the world of private houses, from the eruditely detailed private mansion to the bastardised neo-Georgian estate, clients were not constrained to have what they were told was good for them but bought what they liked: the public voted predominantly for classicism.

In the United States Beaux-Arts classicism soldiered on,

increasingly stripped of ornament, until the Second World War and beyond. The Getty Museum at Malibu, based on the Villa dei Papyri, seems less eccentric when viewed in the context of the Beaux-Arts survival represented by, for instance, the Frick Art Museum in Pittsburg, 1967-70. In inter-War France the language of classicism merged in the the argot of Art Deco.

During the 1930s monumental classicism was seized upon by the Great Dictators as part of their propaganda arsenal. This is not surprising. Classicism has been enrolled in the service of almost every dictator in history; equally, such is the richness of its expressive language that it has embodied the aspirations of some revolutionary democracies. The architecture of the Third Reich does not need to be condemned on grounds of ethics: it was of an aesthetic awfulness almost beyond contemplation. Alas, this is made only too obvious by Leon Krier's recent sumptuous volume on Albert Speer. Italy is a more complicated case. One might have thought that classicism inevitably represented the totalitarian style, but no – Mussolini was equally, if not more captivated by aggressively Modern styles, which he saw as embodying the supposed dynamism of the fascist system. Nevertheless the Duce had classicism both in the blood and on

the Romans; so did Alberti, so did Inigo Jones. Athenian Stuart, Wilkins and Cockerell revived Greece. Often the style that these architects introduced had little in common with what had gone before. Only in retrospect does it seem that they all share something, that they all belong to a common tradition.

Recently some historians have begun to re-evaluate classicism in the 20th century, making both architects and the public feel more comfortable with this aspect of the recent past and perhaps even seeking to establish illusory threads of continuity. Let us look at the British position. A straw in the wind was the acclaimed *Thirties* Exhibition at the Hayward Gallery in 1979. The original intention of the organisers had been to have an architecture section which showed only the Modern Movement, but other historians were so appalled that they were compelled to modify their plan: to the one room showing only the Modern Movement was added another exhibiting the full eclectic range of the decade, and including such works of classicism as M Grey Wornum's RIBA headquarters, Sir John Burnet, Tait and Lorne's Royal Masonic Hospital, Ravenscourt Park, and E Berry Webb's Hammersmith Town Hall.

The same year a major classical building of the 1920s, Sir

QUINLAN TERRY, RICHMOND RIVERSIDE DEVELOPMENT, VIEW OF MODEL

the brain: he vaunted his regime as the natural heir to the Roman Empire. While some of the work of this period is over-inflated and ridiculous, some (Rome University, EUR) is restrained, stylish and haunting – perhaps not as haunting as that of the Metaphysical architects of Milan in the 1920s, however. Led by Muzio, this group developed an elemental classicism which has much in comon with the paintings of De Chirico. But to confuse the ideological picture their sympathies had been communist rather than fascist: what they saw in classicism was the subjugation of self to an external ideal.

Thus many forms of classicism have taken root and flourished at different times this century, demonstrating that there is nothing incompatible between it and our present-day world. Admittedly the tradition cannot yet be read as a continuous one; it is a story of stops and starts. In this country one or two scholarly individuals kept the flame burning through the dark days of the 1950s and 1960s, and they set an example to the architects who came after them. But it is not because of them that the present revival is taking place. That does not matter. The history of classicism is a history of revivals. The Romans revived the Greeks. Charlemagne thought that he was reviving

Edwin Cooper's Old Lloyd's Building in Leadenhall Street, was threatened with demolition. Virtually no one could be found to speak up in its favour. Even Save Britain's Heritage held its peace. There was a widely voiced feeling that it would jeopardise the whole course of contemporary British architecture, and probably the financial viability of the City of London too, if Richard Rogers' replacement – the new Lloyd's – were not allowed to go ahead. The old Lloyd's was demolished, leaving only its richly Piranesian doorcase behind. But the Thirties Society was formed as a result, and since then many hundreds of buildings of the post-1914 period have been listed. Among them is Battersea Power Station, one of the most prominent yet most contentious classical buildings in London which is now being converted to a theme park.

David Watkin's *Morality and Architecture* appeared in 1977. The object of this work, which was controversial at the time, was to undermine the special pleading made on behalf of the Modern Movement; that it was more 'wholesome' or more 'honest' than eclecticism, which had been correspondingly condemned as 'corrupt'. While Watkin was careful not to propose any positive theory of his own in place of 'historicism', his book gave support to traditional Tory values in architecture by the negative means of removing the intellectual crutch on which the opposition had been leaning. In 1979 Watkin's friend Roger Scruton published *The Aesthetics of Architecture*. In the words of the press release issued with it: 'Roger Scruton . . . began his inquiry in 1974 at a time when he felt there was a genuine reaction amongst various architects and thinkers against the values of the modern movement in architecture, and a desire to return to the values of the classical tradition . . . [He] seeks to show how a true understanding of the nature of architecture leads inevitably towards a respect for style, tradition and significant detail.' These ideas were later made more accessible during the period in which he wrote a frequent column for *The Times*.

One of the outstanding phenomena of recent years has been the Lutyens Revival associated with the exhibition on him at the Hayward Gallery in 1981. The organising committee was drawn from the small band of people for whom Lutyens' magic had never tired. It is necessary to emphasise the 'small': he was ignored by many historians because he was out of step with their idea of what the brave new egalitarian, machine-conscious 20th

latter being that on Angiolo Mazzoni in Bologna in 1984. The subject of academic classicism in Germany in these years has, understandably, been treated with greater diffidence because of its promotion by the Nazi regime. But, as the Krier monograph shows, even the work of Speer has recently been taken out of the closet, dusted down and re-presented to the public, though significantly by non-German authors. In the United States the irregularly appearing journal *Classical America*, which has been ploughing a lonely furrow since 1971, has recently been joined by studies on nearly all the major figures in early 20th-century classicism, the most recent being a volume on the uncle after whom Charles Jencks was named, Charles Adam Platt.

Now every architect wants to be classical, just as every politician wants to be considered democratic. This was illustrated during the public inquiry on the tower to Mies van der Rohe designs that Peter Palumbo proposed to build by the Mansion House. Supporters argued that it would complement existing Georgian buildings because it too was classical. As Richard Rogers wrote in his proof of evidence: 'Mies is generally considered to be the greatest classical architect of this century, in fact, the greatest classical architect since Schinkel in the 19th

SIR EDWIN LUTYENS, BRITISH MEDICAL ASSOCIATION, LONDON, 1910

century should have been about. In *An Outline History of European Architecture*, Pevsner omits his name completely. ('It is', comments Watkin, 'like one of those Russian communist photographs from which the presence of some politically unacceptable figure has been skilfully eliminated.') Efforts made to celebrate the centenary of Lutyens' birth in 1969 had been a flop. Funding for the 1981 exhibition was hard to come by, at least to begin with. Yet from the moment it opened, being displayed in a sequence of appropriately articulated rooms by Piers Gough – of which the principal achievement was perhaps to blot out any trace of the Hayward Gallery around them – it met with astounding acclaim from the public and press on both sides of the Atlantic.

In 1982 an exhibition of some of Lutyens' contemporaries in Scandinavia, one of the most fertile regions for classicism until nearly all its practitioners went Modern in about 1930, was organised by authorities in Finland, Sweden, Denmark and Norway. Called *Nordic Classicism, 1910-1930*, it travelled widely and was highly acclaimed. In Italy, scholars led by Cesare de'Seta have confronted Italian work of the 1920s and 1930s in a series of major books and exhibitions – prominent among the

century and possibly since Palladio in the 16th century.' The opponents of the tower were not merely critical but stupefied; they could not believe their ears. To them a high-rise glass tower was manifestly and utterly *un*-classical, and they claimed that this one in particular, not least because of its piazza, would have a catastrophic effect on the neighbourhood. The tower was not built. It is significant that Rogers not only believes Mies to be classical, but such is the weight attached to the great figures of the classical past that he even relates his own architecture – about as calm as an exploding volcano – to Brunelleschi: not the Brunelleschi one first thinks of, the architect of clarity, order and proportion, however, but Brunelleschi the destroyer of the Romanesque/Gothic town for the sake of new planning ideas, Brunelleschi the revolutionary. 'The importance of Brunelleschi is not so much that he rediscovered antiquity and decoratively applied those forms but rather that he developed a new architecture, breaking with the immediate past.' ('Observations on Architecture', in *Richard Rogers and Architects*, 1985, pages 18-19).

The term 'classical' has thus become, in contemporary jargon, 'polyvalent'. An attempt to cut through the layers of ambiguity was made during a dinner given by the Architecture Club in the Royal Institute of British Architects' for the Prince of Wales. Here the theme of the four short speeches and discussion which followed the dinner was: 'Vitruvius, art thou sleeping there below?' Or put another way: what future is there for classical architecture? – a question that could not have been seriously voiced in the RIBA ten years before. One of the speakers, Quinlan Terry, took the definition of classicism as his theme. 'The common man has no doubt in his mind what classicism means', he said. 'It means columns and capitals and cornices; it means pediments and pinnacles; it means architraves and arches and archivolts. But the expert (and I include many here tonight) would say no, it means clean lines, it means a rational disposition of parts, or mental discipline or grain and texture; quite forgetting that all the classical architects of the past employed the Orders, Tuscan, Doric, Ionic, Corinthian and Composite; which for some unaccountable reason they feel to be morally unacceptable or beneath contempt.' Whether or not Terry is right, he has, as always, the enormous advantage of being comprehensible.

Already a surprising quantity of the kind of classical architec-

blowing towards classicism. Krier's scheme was widely acknowledged to be brilliant: Continental rationalist in its analysis of function and its hierarchy of building types; English Picturesque in the varied streetscape that it would have produced. It is London's loss that he was not able to carry it through. He handed over to Quinlan Terry whose own, very different scheme was rejected by the City Corporation in favour of an amorphous megastructure which will be built by another property company.

The third scheme is John Simpson's for Paternoster Square. It does not have a chance of being built; it never did have, since it was not commissioned by the Paternoster Consortium and did not follow their brief. However it is significant in that it embodies the views of the Prince of Wales. The Prince, with his dream that Britain can still be made beautiful again, is a force that no one should fail to reckon with. His genius in his architectural comments is not for originality, but, on the contrary, for giving voice to the views that many ordinary people have long felt and expressed but which have not been heard by the profession. If he is set to champion classicism, it is yet another sign that its hour has come.

L TO R: JOHN SIMPSON, PATERNOSTER SQUARE PROPOSAL, 1987; C B COCKERELL, SUN ASSURANCE OFFICE, LONDON, 1841

ture that would pass Terry's definition is now being built. Much, but not all, is for private clients. Three schemes stand out as pointing the way to the future. The first is Terry's own £20 million Richmond Riverside development. It was undertaken for Haslemere Estates, which was unfortunately purchased by a Dutch company shortly after construction began. The buildings – mixed terraces, to accommodate a steeply sloping site dotted with listed structures that had to be retained – are now coming out of their scaffolding, and it is already easy to predict what the response will be: mealy-mouthed disapproval from the critics, instant and overwhelming success with the public. Richmond Riverside is the largest classical project in Britain since the Second World War. Its popularity with the public is assured. But the importance of the scheme is that it demonstrates that classicism works not only for private houses but in the tough commercial marketplace of speculative office development. The second scheme, Leon Krier's for the Spitalfields Market site, will never be built but it illustrates a tendency, for it was commissioned by Rosehaugh Stanhope, backed by some of the most powerful property developers in the business. They know which way the wind is blowing and here they decided that it was

Clive Aslet is Architectural Editor of Country Life, *and the author of several books, including* The Last Country Houses, The National Trust Book of the English House, *and, most recently,* Quinlan Terry: The Revival of Architecture.

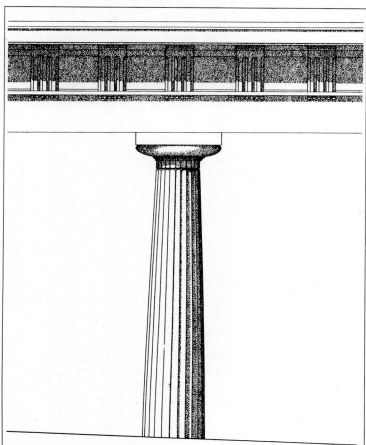

DETAILS FOR COLONNADE, *CLOCKWISE FROM TOP LEFT:* DORIC, TUSCAN, CORINTHIAN, GREEK DORIC

Both resolutions were provoked by Viet-   possess it.

car for sparing
care for future
provision

VICTORIAN VALUES

Being sober

One of the charges continually urged against Mrs Thatcher is that she is trying to reimpose "Victorian values" on the British people. But what are "Victorian values"? And what, this question answered, is wrong with reimposing them?

These matters are addressed in a pamphlet published today by the Centre for Policy Studies, the independent research and publishing organization which exists to support the case for responsible capitalism and over which the Prime Minister herself continues to preside, though in no way by virtue of her office. The pamphlet is by Professor Gertrude Himmelfarb, a distinguished historian, and it makes its point instantly in the words of its title: *"Victorian Values and Twentieth-Century Condescension"*. *(patronizing manner)*

Essentially, what the 20th century thinks about the ethical principles for which the Victorians are supposed to have stood is that they were invented by a triumphant middle class for the purpose of beating the poor into submission. Their aim, it is believed, was to attribute all social evils to the fecklessness, sexual incontinence and drunkeness of the urban multitude. From the effects of these vices the poor could only be saved by the providence, restraint, sobriety and compassion of the rich and by diligent attempts to emulate these virtues themselves and meantime to accept with patience and humility the consequences of their condition. It is this parody of the culture of Victorian England, produced largely by Marxist analysis which Professor Himmelfarb sets out to correct.

The core of her argument is contained in this passage:"To the degree to which Victorians succeeded in 'bourgeoisifying' the ethos, they also democratised it. That ethos was not, to be

ineffcient, feckless people

sure, an exalted or heroic one. Hard work, sobriety, frugality, foresight — these were modest, mundane virtues, even lowly ones. But they were virtues within the capacity of everyone; they did not assume any special breeding, or status, or talent, or valour, or grace — or even money. They were common virtues within the reach of common people. They were, so to speak, democratic virtues."

In other words, Victorian morality in matters economic was the common property of the nation; its aim was not to enslave the poor, but to liberate them. To dismiss it as one huge con, is an act of condescension not only towards the Victorians but towards the working classes themselves.

It is easy to see how Mrs Thatcher fits into this picture. To put it in Marxist terms, she also wishes to "universalize the middle-classes". She wants them to own their own houses, to have a far larger degree of choice about the education of their children, and to be able to buy and sell shares. It is a peculiarly perverse line of argument which suggests that this is a recipe for enslavement rather than liberation, that its purpose is to preserve class distinctions rather than to diminish them and that it represents a social ideal markedly inferior to that presented by the principal alternative on offer.

That alternative is the belief that the vast majority of the people are incapable of those modest Victorian virtues which are essential to the well-being of a property owning society and that the mass of mankind must therefore be the objects of compassion and patronage on the part of their rulers. The essential merit of "Victorian Mrs Thatcher" is that she does not patronize the people.

Foresight
timely care — providence

SRI LANKAN ACCORD

The peace accord intended to end the ethnic conflict in Sri Lanka is beginning to take effect. Barring a few unconfirmed incidents hostilities

conditions the Tamils wrung out of the Indian Government was that Indian soldiers would form the peace keeping force which will

Andrews and Edinburgh, 77; Lord Kahn, 82; Mr Leonard Lickorish, former director-general British Tourist Authority, 66; Lord Lisle, 84; Miss Kate O'Mara, actress, 48; Lord Porritt, 87; Sir Stanley Raymond, former chairman, British Railways Board, 74; Mrs Elizabeth Thomas, literary consultant, 68; Major-General Sir Humphry Tollemache, 90; Mr W.T. Wells, QC, former MP, 79; Sir John Spencer Wills, former chairman, British Electric Traction Company, 83; Mr P.H. Wright, VC, 71; Mr George Wynn-Williams, obstetrician and gynaecologist, 75.

Today's royal engagements

The Duke of York, accompanied by the Duchess of York, will take the salute at the 1987 Cardiff Tattoo at Cardiff Castle at 7.05.

The Princess Royal, Patron of the Royal Lymington Yacht Club, will attend the club's junior regatta at Lymington, Hampshire, at 10.00.

Royal Society of St George

The following have been elected officers of the Royal Society of St George for the ensuing year: President, Lieutenant-Colonel Sir Colin Cole; Chairman, Mr John Minshull-Fogg; Vice-Chairman, Mr George Andrews.

Service dinner

Leciestershire and Northamptonshire ACF
The Lord Lieutenant of Leicestershire and the Lord Lieutenant of Northamptonshire were among the guests at a dinner given by Colonel J.M.K. Weir, County Commandant, and officers of the Leicestershire and Northamptonshire Army Cadet Force at Wathgill Camp, Yorkshire, on Saturday.

and masked a hankering afte a more authoritarian order and what they regarded as a more authentic Japanese tradition.

Kishi formed his first Cabinet in 1957, at the early age (for Japan) of 60. He immediately gave the new administration the impress of his views and personality. Whereas his predecessors had laid stress on Japan's relations with her Communist neighbours, Kishi made the alliance with the United States the cornerstone of his policy.

He launched a vigorous economic offensive in South-East Asia.

In domestic policy the Government pursued revisionist

democracy back towards the authoritarian State of pre-war years - has more than a grain of truth. At the same time it should be remembered that he was firmly pro-American and anti-Communist.

But his most lasting legacy may have been a negative one. The scale and violence of the crisis of 1960 shook Japan's political establishment to its core. Kishi's style of government came to be seen as having been needlessly provocative. His successors preferred to rest their appeal on the proven ability of the economy to create ever-increasing wealth rather than to engage in dangerous political adventurism.

MR HARRY BROWN

Mr Harry Brown, who made a successful career out of publishing lively financial advice for the large number of British people who go overseas to work or retire, died in Jersey on July 24. He was 53.

His skill was in translating intricacies like the rules on double taxation into readable language, and leavening them with snippets of non-financial advice for those who exchange life in an English suburb for villa life in places in the sun; keep your underwear in the refrigerator, he suggested.

In the 1970s, Brown contributed articles to *The Times* addressed to people taking a job abroad. The volume of requests that flowed in for more information showed the

need for advice for pensioners. He was concerned less with wealthy "tax exiles" than with "those who have worked hard all their lives and who for one reason or another decide to make a move to a more temperate climate, a lower rate of inflation or simply a change of scene to meet their plans for retirement."

His best-known book was *Brits Abroad*, which he was revising for a new edition at the time of his death. He also wrote *Working Abroad?* and *Retiring Abroad?*

He had lectured extensively around the world, broadcast here and abroad and produced a monthly newspaper for expatriates.

MAJOR LEONARD DENT

T. G. writes:
No memorial to Leonard Dent (obituary, July 24) can be complete without reference to one of the overriding interests and loves of his life — the City and Guilds of London

integrity of the school caused him to campaign, eventually with success, for its complete autonomy.

Those who had the happy privilege of being led into these battles by Leonard will

QUINLAN TERRY
Richmond Riverside Development

VIEW OF MODEL FROM BRIDGE STREET

Quinlan Terry's largest urban project to date is for mixed commercial usage, unlike most of his work, which has been for private country houses. The design therefore needed to take into consideration its location in a prominent historic site on the River Thames and the character of Richmond as a residential, shopping and recreational centre, and to show that Terry's style could be used in a modern, economic context.

Scheduled for completion in Spring 1988, the development is primarily office space, providing approximately 106,000 sq ft but there will also be 10,600 sq ft for retail use, plus two restaurants, 28 flats, and underground parking.

Rather than one large building, Terry has produced a series of separate, but linked, houses ranged round three squares with landscaping down to the river, and arcaded walkways on the Bridge

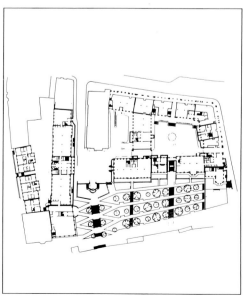

SITE PLAN

Street and Hill Street frontages. The separate elements give the project a domestic feel. They also simplified construction on a sloping site; were suitable for the medium-sized office units the developers wanted; allowed a variety of classical styles under an overall unity of scheme; and enabled the restoration of some existing buildings within the complex. On the river frontage, Tower House (remodelled as a restaurant), Palm and Heron Houses remain amongst the new Link Building, with its Palladian gateway to Town Square, and Hotham House, a large, pedimented block with roof cupola.

Construction is in traditional load-bearing brick with a high standard of finishing. As usual, Terry has paid great attention to classical details, such as cupolas, window surrounds, decorative finials and the different Orders, but making economical use of reconstituted stone.

11

Photos: Mark Fiennes

DECORATIVE DETAILS

DECORATIVE DETAILS

THE ERECHTHEION, PORTICO OF THE CARYATIDS, DETAIL

DEMETRI PORPHYRIOS
Imitation & Convention in Architecture

STOA OF ATTALOS, ATHENS, DOOR DETAIL

Whenever we visit or look at a building, we find our attention moving in two directions at once. One is pragmatic, and concerned with how the building functions. The other has to do with the nature of the building; in other words, we see the building as something that has been made. This is so since in human fabrication, in general, significance lies not in the utility or beauty that may accompany the artifact but in the recognition of ourselves as the makers of that artifact.

This recognition is essentially a contemplative experience and, when viewed like this, the building – though it may be useful – refuses to be used in any way. Architecture begins precisely here; it speaks of the usefulness which produced it in the first place, from which it detaches itself as art and to which it always alludes.

We may therefore ask: what is the nature and purpose of this detachment and what are the means by which it is achieved? In other words, in what sense can we say that

POSTCARD OF FLAMENCO DANCERS

architecture detaches itself from the contingencies of shelter and construction and, if so, why and how does it do that?

*   *   *

The conception of architecture (and art in general) as having a relationship to contingent reality which is not direct but potential, can be traced back to Greek antiquity. In his *Poetics*, Aristotle discusses poetry and art as a form of truth liberated from experience: a response awakened in the observer by the transformation of experience and contingent reality into fictitious play. The central principle of Aristotelian aesthetics is that art is the imitation of nature. But what exactly are we to understand by the expression 'imitation of nature'?

The term 'imitation' has been so much used and misused in literary and popular discussion that its original Aristotelian meaning has been virtually lost. Already by the Hellenistic and Roman periods,

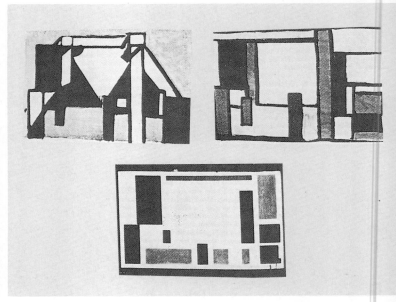

L To R: K F SCHINKEL, *THE BIRTH OF PAINTING*; THEO VAN DOESBURG, *NEOPLASTIC PRINCIPLES*

the *Poetics* was not widely known and the major commentary which had taken its place was Horace's *Ars Poetica*. Working within a Hellenistic framework of thought that favoured the art of rhetoric, Horace distinguished between style and content and emphasised the former at the expense of the latter. The preservation of Aristotle's text was ultimately due to the literary cultures of Islam and Byzantium. The first printed edition of the *Poetics* appeared in Venice in 1508, and from then on a number of translations and commentaries were published during the Renaissance. Later, Neo-classicism turned the *Poetics* into codified, normative principles, at the same time elevating art into an idealised, metaphysical realm. With the advent of 19th-century romantic theories of genius. imagination and subjectivity, the *Poetics* lost its appeal, and by the time Brecht contrasted Dramatic and Epic theatre most of Aristotle's original ideas were forgotten. In fact Brecht did what was expected of him by his time: he associated the *Poetics* with naturalistic, outmoded ideology and thereby dismissed it without being prepared to understand it.

In a certain sense Brecht was right in suspecting the *Poetics* of

outmoded clichés – Aristotle's text had been so often associated with the generalisation 'art imitates nature' or other similar statements found in Renaissance treatises on poetry, art and architecture. In fact, similar commonplaces are still current today and I suspect that is why in everyday language the word imitation brings to mind cloned replicas. Given our century's preoccupation with modern art, one can understand how such a naturalistic theory of art might appear suspect.

It is true that in his *Poetics* Aristotle writes that 'art imitates nature' (e techne mimeitai ten phusin). But this could not possibly have the sense that art is a reproduction of natural objects, since nature for Aristotle is not the physical world that surrounds us but rather the active force of the universe. Indeed the inadequacy of the English translation 'imitation' for the Aristotelian mimesis can be shown by a passage in the *Poetics* where it is mentioned that the artist 'imitates things as they ought to be' (oia einai thei). This passage shows clearly that imitation (mimesis) does *not* refer to a literal transcription of the world. It does *not* denote the servile duplication of the model; it is neither a copy nor a simulation of the physical world that

L TO R: AGAMEMNON'S TOMB, MYCENAE; G ASPLUND, STOCKHOLM LIBRARY

L TO R: LE CORBUSIER, VILLA SAVOYE, ENTRANCE HALL; G ASPLUND, ENSKEDE CREMATORIUM, FOUNTAIN OF ABLUTION

surrounds us.

To imitate things as they *ought to be* means to represent something in a way that allows us to come closer to knowing it. Artistic imitation, in the Aristotelian sense, reveals the artist's (and our own as observers) preoccupations, concerns and criteria of evaluation. In that sense an imitation of the world is always a transformation of the world, since what we select to represent through the work of art is necessarily what we have deemed to be relevant for representation.

An etymological nuance throws further light on the Aristotelian concept of mimesis. We read in the *Poetics* that the artist imitates '*things as they ought to be*' (the italics are mine). Surely Aristotle does not have in mind here 'things' as mere physical objects. Heidegger has pointed out that the old German word for *thing* 'becomes the name for an affair or matter of pertinence. In fact, the meaning of the Greek word for thing (pragma, from prattein, that which has been acted upon and therefore rendered pertinent) is still preserved in the English word as when we say, "he knows how to handle things" – he knows how to deal with what matters.'

The meaning of Aristotle is clear. The artist imitates things as they ought to be (and therefore not necessarily as they are in the real world). What is more, he imitates no physical objects as such but rather 'things' in so far as they are the vehicles of an essential significance to him. It is in this sense that we can say that the Aristotelian concept of mimesis shows the way in which the world is true for us.

Consider for a moment Hume, who writes that 'the rules of architecture require that the top of a pillar should be more slender than its base . . . because such a figure conveys to us the idea of security . . .' (*A Treatise on Human Nature*, II, I, iii). The entasis of a column does not follow the exact profile of the tree trunk. It comprises an image of nature's visual statics.

Consider also Le Corbusier: 'Let us reflect for a moment on the fact that there is nothing in nature that . . . approaches the pure perfection of the humblest machine: the tree trunk is not straight . . . If we say with certainty that nature is geometrical it is not that we have seen it; it is rather that we have interpreted it in accordance with our own framework' ('The Lesson of the Machine' in *L'Art décoratif d'aujourd'hui*). The Corbusian *pilo-*

L TO R: M G BINDESBØLL, THORVALDSENS MUSEUM; K F SCHINKEL, CHARLOTTENHOF, POTSDAM

tis comprise an image of nature's geometricity by analogy with the machine.

In these examples, both Hume and Le Corbusier speak of the way the column imitates the tree. Neither of the two speak of actually imitating a tree. Hume discovers in nature's workings an anthropomorphic image. Le Corbusier, on the other hand, discovers in nature a geometricity which is made pertinent by his admiration for the precision and exactitude of the machine. The classical imagination looks at the tree trunk and sees in it an image of stability, which it commemorates in the form of the entasis of the column. Le Corbusier, aspiring to the attainment of mechanical geometricity, sees the tree trunk as a precise cylindrical form.

In both cases the artist imitates no physical objects as such, but rather 'things' in so far as they have an essential significance for him. From one artist to another (or between different historical periods) the significance brought forward might vary and indeed it does; yet all art is imitation in the sense of representing the relevance that some-'thing' has for us. It is in this sense that we should understand the Aristotelian concept of

we can say that a work of art is a likeness of the model. A painting of a landscape does not use leaves and shrubbery but simply paint. A sculpture of a maiden does not use the maiden in flesh, nor does it attempt to render the folds of her dress in real cloth. Similarly in architecture, a column does not render the bark of the tree with the moss growing on it. This is an obvious point and yet, so often, we tend to forget the necessary 'distance' that artistic likeness demands. I am reminded here of a postcard I once saw in Spain, a colour photograph depicting two flamenco dancers. Its author must have found the photographic impression wanting and, eager to 'enrich' it, he added real lace for the lady's skirt and silk for her blouse. Somewhere, I am sure, there must be an 'improvement' of this postcard where the castanets can be heard aloud and the aroma of the Sevillian dusk touched our nostrils.

We know of course that this is kitsch. For what is kitsch if not a hallucinatory promise of the world in flesh 'inducing a hedonistic relaxation as a compensatory strategy' (Adorno). The difference between kitsch and art is that kitsch simulates as a compensation for that which is not; art imitates in order to distance itself

L TO R: SHED IN THE ENVIRONS OF BOLOGNA; SHED IN TUSCANY

imitation. Mimesis (imitation) discloses the way by which the world is true for us.

*　　*　　*

In what fashion does art speak to us? What are the means by which artistic imitation discloses the truth of the world for us? Does the work of art appeal to reason? Does it describe the world with concepts and discursive language? Aristotle reminds us here that a work of art is neither science nor philosophy but a likeness (homeioma) of some-'thing' found in the world.

Of the issues arising from the notion of artistic likeness, three demand special attention. In the first place, the notion of likeness points out that the work of art is always rendered in a sensuous medium (for example, paint, marble, sound, etc) and therefore speaks to us through the senses and not through the intellect. Art and architecture do not reach us by means of abstract reason but through our senses. Their medium is not discursive thought but sensuous form.

Secondly, in so far as the artistic medium is materially different from that in which its model is fashioned in the first place,

from that which is and thereby throw new light on to it. This distancing is not a sign of ineptitude on the part of the artist but rather, a crucial characteristic of artistic production as such. By distancing himself from his model, the artist forces us to see what we have never seen before, pointing out a relevance that might otherwise have gone unnoticed. What the work shows is elicited from contingent reality and is brought forward for our contemplation. There is enough resemblance with the model for us to understand what the work refers to; the rest is all 'truth'. To continue with our previous examples: the entasis of a classical column makes us see, in the diminishing girth of a tree trunk, nature's law of stability; on the other hand, the cylindrical form of the Corbusian column makes us see a projected geometricity of nature and thereby the machine as *bella natura*. Art and architecture construct a new world by both preserving and cancelling out the contingent world of our everyday life. The artist imitates the world by distancing himself from it and thereby discloses the way in which the world is true for him. If or when, we find such truth relevant to ourselves, we rejoice and call the work beautiful.

The third aspect of the notion of aesthetic likeness concerns the common understanding of likeness as *trompe l'oeil* illusionism. In naturalistic theories of art it is assumed that the excellence of a painting corresponds to the faithfulness with which a painted representation matches the reality. Pliny, for example, records the story of the contest between Parrhasius and Zeuxis. The latter painted a bunch of grapes and birds flocked to peck them. Parrhasius then painted a curtain so realistically that he deceived Zeuxis, who asked for it to be drawn so that he might see the picture behind. Similarly Vasari tells the story of the young Giotto who painted a fly on to a picture by his master Cimabue so convincingly that Cimabue was deceived and made a gesture to drive the fly away.

Imitation – in the classical Aristotelian sense – has nothing to do with this idea of illusionistic likeness. From the outset artistic imitation abjures the satisfaction of merely naturalistic depiction. It does not aim at deception. Not for a moment does artistic imitation leave us in doubt about the fact that it intends to portray what is essential, not merely what is naturalistic. Imitation (the likeness of) does not involve the false belief that we are

alludes. The form of the classical architrave makes us recognise the universal law of gravity and stability. In fact, recognising some-'thing' means knowing what is universal and essential. Recognition is the experience of familiarity with the world, not simply as a collection of contingent objects and events, but as an intelligible narative. Thus, 'the reason why men enjoy seeing a likeness', writes Aristotle, 'is that in contemplating it they find themselves learning or inferring and saying perhaps, "Ah, that is he"'.

* * *

It is this emotional delight accompanying the pleasure of recognition of what is true for us that becomes the chief factor in the enjoyment of the arts. The theory of imitation (mimesis) seems to suggest, therefore, that art and architecture is a form of knowledge that serves to deepen our understanding of ourselves and thus our familiarity with the world. Let me pause for a moment and take stock of what we have said thus far:

1 Artistic imitation does *not* denote the servile duplication of the model; it is neither a copy nor a simulation.
2 The artist imitates things as they ought to be; that is, he

DEMETRI PORPHYRIOS

L. TO R: BREMO HOUSE, VIRGINIA; SHED IN THE ENVIRONS OF BOLOGNA

the actual presence of what an image represents. Instead, we approach the work of art as an image (phantasma, likeness) of the world which the artist has judged to be especially worth commemorating.

The work of art exists as a bridge between the example and the precept. It represents a universal truth (ta katholou) by imitating particular examples chosen for their typicality (ta kath' ekaston). This is not to say that a general idea is embodied in a particular example, but that the particular case is generalised by artistic treatment. No doubt this is the meaning of Goethe when he writes that 'a special case requires nothing but the treatment of a poet to become universal'.

The classical architrave generalises the otherwise particular and contingent experience of post and lintel construction. The aim here is not to reproduce the lintel itself as a structural member with its sectional dimensions and material properties specified by the engineer, for that would be a symbolically mute gesture. Instead, the form of the classical architrave makes us see the structural members which produced it in the first place, from which it has detached itself as art and to which it always

represents what he has deemed relevant for representation. Artistic imitation, therefore, is a transformation of the world.
3 The artist imitates no physical objects as such but rather 'things' in so far as they have a significance for him. In that sense, artistic imitation discloses the way in which the world is true for us.
4 The work of art is always a likeness of some'thing' found in the world.
a A work of art is a likeness in so far as it always uses sensuous form as its medium and never employs intellectual or discursive language.
b A work of art is a likeness insofar as it is rendered in a medium that is materially different from that in which the model is fashioned in the first place. This introduces a necessary and telling distance from the model.
c A work of art is a likeness not in the sense of *trompe l'oeil* illusionism but of a categorical order. The work of art exists as a bridge between the example and the precept. The work of art represents a universal truth by imitating particular examples.
5 The aim (purpose) of art and architecture is to afford an

emotional delight that accompanies the pleasure of recognition of what is true for us.

* * *

The artist shows us, in sensuous form, a representation of some-'thing' found in the world. This always involves establishing a distance from the model. It is exactly this distance which gives significance and truth to the work of art.

It is the distance which separates the timber shed from the temple that gives classical architecture its significance as a commemoration of shelter, construction and the laws of nature. It is the distance which separates the real cow from that painted by Van Doesburg that makes the painting a canonic statement of the primacy of objective, abstract essences. The theory of imitation (mimesis) is at the core of both traditional and modern art.

I have spoken of the relations that artistic imitation establishes between the work of art and the world. But what about the relations between one work of art and another? It is obvious that like a painting, a statue, a sonata or a poem, a building is one of a class of similar forms. To understand what classical architecture

are unaccustomed to the conventions of a country they do not stand out. The same is true with the conventions of art and architecture.

Today, however, the conventional element in architecture is elaborately disguised; first by the Modernist slogan 'down with conventions; long live the free spirit of experimentation'. Though such slogans were useful to the movement in the 1920s, they became meaningless once Modern architecture had established itself. There have been, of course, a few for whom modernity had meant a permanent state of crisis. According to this view architecture is always *in extremis.* But even when we examine the recent deconstructionist mood of transgression and de-simulation of excremental culture, we come across numerous conventions which, while admittedly perhaps short-lived, are necessary for the production of any work. In fact, deconstruction does not deny the conventional element; it cannot, by its very own definition. It simply suspends the view that conventions are meaningful in order to see what happens when the tacit assumptions of convention no longer run.

In that sense today's Neo-Modernists are no different from

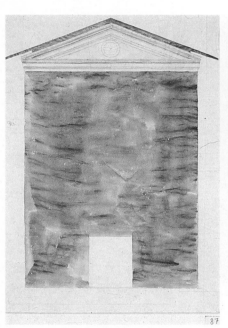  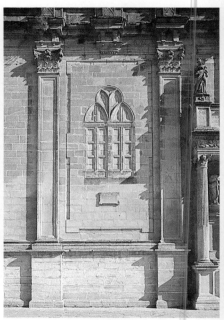

L TO R: S LEWERENTZ, CHAPEL OF THE RESURRECTION; D PORPHYRIOS, PROPYLON, SURREY; VESTIGIAL WINDOW CARVED IN STONE, UBEDA, SPAIN

is, therefore, takes us beyond the discussion of the imitative relations that bind the timber shed to the temple. We have to ask the question of the relations of one classical building to another and with this idea two considerations become important: *convention* and *originality.*

The study of conventions is based on analogies of form. It is clear that any classical building (and this applies equally to all classic architecture we speak of as enduring) may be studied not only as an imitation of the world and construction, but as an imitation of other classical buildings as well. Virgil discovered, Pope reminds us, that imitating nature was ultimately the same thing as imitating Homer. Once we think of a classical building in relation to other classical buildings, we can see that a great part of creative design addresses the formation and transformation of conventions.

All art and architecture is equally conventionalised, but we do not notice this as such conventions are always meant to appear natural and universal, otherwise their authority and role as the binding 'cement' of society would be undermined. In fact, conventions can best be studied when one travels, for unless we

the Post-Modernists. They both thrive on convention: the first by dismembering conventions in the name of deconstructionist critique; the second by saturating the market with 'instant conventions' in the name of pluralism. I never understood why Jencks has kept the Neo-Modernists at a distance, denying them a slice of the Post-Modern cake. Very soon he will realise this and by 'discovering' them he will give to Post-Modernism a few more years of life.

There is another factor that disguises the importance of the conventional element in architecture: copyright laws. As we all know, the market ethic of the original and authentic is based on the pretence that every work of art is an invention singular enough to be patented. As a consequence of this frame of mind, demonstrating the debt of Giulio Romano to Bramante is today called scholarship, but it would be denounced as plagiarism were Giulio Romano still alive.

Ironically, this state of things would make it difficult to appraise an architecture which includes, say, Palladio, much of whose architecture is paraphrased from others, or Schinkel whose buildings sometimes follow their sources almost verbatim. If for a moment we move to poetry, I am reminded of Milton who asked for nothing better than to borrow the whole of the Bible.

It is unfortunate, but true, that it is not only the inexperienced Modern architect who looks for a residual originality as a hallmark of talent. Most of us today tend to think of an architect's real achievement as having nothing to do with the achievement present in what he borrowed. We therefore tend to concentrate on peripheral issues of personal stylistics or *maniera*. But let us think for a moment of the greatness of, say, Alberti. His greatness lies in the fact that he gave a new lease of life to the humanist theme itself, passing it on to the 15th century from the sources of antiquity.

Let me qualify this observation to avoid misapprehension. The distance between a new work and the model that has inspired it is indeed always the hallmark of creative talent, pointing out the contemporaneity of the work. But at the same time we have to realise that the conception of a great architect entrusted with a heritage must be as elementary to us as it was to Alberti. And yet such an attitude would seem to violate the

novels – that is all OK and human. But architecture is not made out of these things. Buildings can only be made out of other buildings. Architecture shapes itself. Its forms can no more exist outside architecture than the form of a sonata can exist outside music.

Any serious study of architecture (and art in general) soon shows that the real difference between the great and the lesser architect is that the former imitates the principles of a great heritage, unlike the latter who copies the mannerisms of his predecessors or his contemporaries. That is the true meaning of creativity and originality. Whereas, if creativity is to be understood as production *ex nihilo*, there would soon be no place for competence and intelligence and we should then not be surprised if schools and professional bodies set up 'creativity tests'!

* * *

The subject of imitation and convention raises the question of how architecture can be meaningful. Architecture as one of the aspects of civilisation is concerned with recurrent images that afford recognition of the world. The roof, the truss, the portico,

DISSOLUTION AND CELEBRATION OF TECTONICS: SPANISH BAROQUE; HOUSE IMPRINTED ON WALLS OF CASTIGLION FIORENTINO; K F SCHINKEL, CHARLOTTENBURG PAVILION

prejudices about 'creation *ex nihilo*' that most of us are educated in today.

Historically, of course, we have been told to believe that this 'fall from grace' was triggered by the profound change in the social position of the artist/architect after the middle of the 18th century. He gradually lost the patronage of the Church, the State and the aristocracy that had sustained him for centuries, and found himself confronted with an anonymous and frequently uneducated public. This new client, we are told, he openly despised. At the same time the artist demanded the public's approval even when it could not understand his art. This 19th century romantic attitude had much to do with the Modernist slogan of 'down with conventions' and is still with us today, especially among those Neo-Modern aesthetes of a deconstructionist persuasion.

But it is hardly possible to accept a view which imagines that a creative architect stares at a white board and designs *ex nihilo*. Human beings do *not* create in that way. Architecture may employ technology and it may be implicated with social and economic parameters; architects might read philosophy and

the column, the ochre or white-washed wall, the brick pergola opening up to the garden, all connect one building with another and help make intelligible our architectural experience of the world. Through the technique of imitation architecture raises itself above the mere contingencies of building and sets symbols for recognition. By means of convention these symbols are composed, varied and re-composed in an ever-changing chain of variations. Yet always the aim is to make man come to terms with the world. The role of imitation and convention in architecture is to elicit that which is lasting and true for us from the transient.

Note

All quotations from Aristotle are from his *Poetics*, MSS Parisinus 2038, English translation by S H Butcher, *Aristotle's Theory of Poetry and Fine Art*.

1 FREART DE CHAMBRAY, *PARALLÈLE DE L'ARCHITECTURE ANTIQUE AVEC LA MODERNE*, PARIS, 1650

CHARLES JENCKS
The New Classicism & its Emergent Rules

2 ANUBIS SHRINE, HATSHEPUT'S TEMPLE, c1500 BC: CAVETTO MOULDING AND PROTO-DORIC COLUMNS

The third phase of Post-Modernism, which started in the late 1970s, has led to a new form of classicism, a free-style rather than canonic version of the traditional language. Many people misunderstand it, and not a few criticise what they take to be its mistakes or licence. But like all fundamental shifts in cultural forms – especially such well-established ones – it asks to be understood on its own terms according to new emergent canons or rules. It is true this free-style classicism shares

some traditional assumptions with previous revivals, most importantly the idea of relating our efforts to those of the past, and using universal figures of representation, or previously discovered constants of a language. The portrayal of the human body in art and the figurative use of the column in architecture are the two most obvious constants to have reappeared under new guises, but one could easily extend this list to cover 20 or more similar elements, compositional rules and qualities. Thus the new classicism has appeared partly because those creating it have rediscovered necessity: the fact that if archetypes and universals are inevitable, they might as well be consciously articulated or turned into a representational art.

The motives for the hybrid mode vary, but they force us to look at the past in a new way and to come to terms with the fact, suppressed in discussions of classical architecture, that its roots are Egyptian, not just Greek and Roman (2, 3). The Egyptians invented most of the elements of stone architecture, including the syntactic rules for combining them, and they practised a symbolic and hybrid mode which relates directly to that of today. Underlying all these motives is the idea that, in its continuous evolution, the classical language has been transformed over time and ties generations together in a common pursuit. Artists and architects who work on archetypal problems will naturally come to related solutions, which serve to pull history together into a continuum and even, on a cultural level, make history reversible.

The Reversible Historical Continuum

The revival of classicism has often been accompanied by personal testament, or a description of a private endeavour between friends. Indeed one of its most surprising aspects is this expression of self-disclosure and individual commitment. This was particularly true in the Renaissance which, as its root-meaning suggests, was always concerned with spiritual rebirth. Antonio Filarete, the architect and sculptor, describes the characteristic experience of conversion, quite naturally, using the metaphor of personal, spiritual reawakening, writing in 1460:

I, too, used to like modern [*scil., Gothic*] buildings, but when I began to appreciate classical ones, I came to be disgusted with the former . . . Having heard that the people of Florence had started in this classical manner [*a questi modi antichi*], I decided to get hold of one of those . . . and when I associated with them, they woke me up in such a way that now I could not produce that smallest thing in any manner but the classical . . . I seem to see, my lord [in the new structures built according to the *modi antichi*] those noble edifices that existed in Rome in classical times and those that, we read, existed in Egypt; I appear to be reborn when I see these noble edifices, and they seem still beautiful to me.[1]

Filarete uses a confessional, private tone of voice. As Erwin Panofsky points out, the renaissance of classicism is associated with a personal 'reawakening', a 'restoration', '*rinascita*', 'resur-

23

rection' or 'second birth'. This ultimately goes back to the Gospel of St John: 'Except a man be born again, he cannot see the kingdom of God.' The born-again Christian of today has his secular counterpart in the born-again classicist. The implications are interesting. When an architect or painter suddenly recognises the Western tradition as a *living alternative* to the Modernist notion of the 'tradition of the new' and realises that his efforts can play a part within it, he can experience a rebirth similar to that felt by the born-again Christian. This is one idea of classicism which links architects, artists and writers today. Such an insight leads to a personal disclosure because it is self-conscious: the architect and painter suddenly understand the classical tradition not merely as an endless set of forms and motifs, but as an idea that is alive. The consciousness of this idea leads to a personal challenge.

Again, the testimonies from the Italian Renaissance bring out this challenge. 'After I had returned from exile', Alberti writes in his preface to *Della Pittura*, 1435, 'I recognised in many, but foremost in you, Filippo [Brunelleschi], and in that very good friend of ours, Donato the sculptor, and in . . . Massacio, a genius for all praiseworthy endeavour not inferior to that of the

idea. Hence the disputes as to what should be included. Where did the form come from, who developed and perfected it, what are its historical meanings? Classicism is always involved with a heightened historical consciousness. The Greeks knew Egypt well, and we may term their transformation of Egyptian architecture 'the first classical revival'. As Filarete reveals, the Renaissance also recognised its debt to Egypt.

The concept of an artistic community in continuity has led some writers to follow the extreme formulation of this idea by T S Eliot, an author who regarded himself as a classicist in literature. He also saw the Western tradition as an organic continuum – a reversible, living entity whose *past* could be changed by the introduction of a new link in the chain. It's a potent idea and one that has deservedly changed the way we think about the classical tradition and its necessary dependence on true innovation:

Tradition is a matter of much wider significance. It cannot be inherited, and if you want it you must obtain it by great labour. It involves, in the first place, the historical sense . . . the historical sense compels a man to write not merely with his own generation in his bones, but with a feeling that

3 HATSHEPUT'S MORTURAY TEMPLE, DEIR EL-BAHARI, c1500 BC: FREE-STYLE CLASSICAL MOTIFS

famous ancients . . .'[2] The friends of Alberti are being called together on a first-name basis ('you, Filippo') to challenge the ancients in a way that will not only revive those dead artists, but revivify these living ones.

When the moderns are put on the same level as the ancients, two things happen. Firstly, time becomes reversible and historical figures live and become equal to contemporary ones. Secondly, this equality between old and new artists soon leads, as it did in the 17th century, to protracted comparisons and then finally to an attempt to find winners and losers in the competition for ideal classical form (1). The famous quarrel of the 'Ancients' and 'Moderns' which took place within the French Academy in the 1670s led to the later 'battle of the styles', a struggle between Modernists of all brands that is still with us today. But the positive aspect of this struggle should be stressed – the notion of the classical tradition as an organic continuum, a living whole.

Partly, this idea is nothing more than a practical insight: each generation learns from preceding ones, taking some of its values and formal solutions and passing them on to the future. Hence the pedigree, or provenance, always entailed in the classical

the whole of the literature of Europe from Homer and within it the whole of the literature of his own country has a simultaneous existence and composes a simultaneous order . . . No poet, no artist of any art, has his complete meaning alone. His significance, his appreciation is the appreciation, of his relation to the dead poets and artists. You cannot value him alone; you must set him, for contrast and comparison, among the dead. . .what happens when a new work of art is created is something that happens simultaneously to all the works of art which preceded it. The existing monuments form an ideal order among themselves, which is modified by the introduction of the new . . . work of art among them. The existing order is complete before the new work arrives; for order to persist after the supervention of novelty, the whole existing order must be, if ever so slightly, altered; and so the relations, proportions, values of each work of art toward the whole are readjusted; and this is conformity between the old and the new. Whoever has approved this idea of order, of the form of European, of English literature, will not find it preposterous that the past should be altered by the present as much as the present is directed by the past . . .[3]

This organic tradition certainly does work on a metaphorical and perceptual level: we change our view of the past through new creations in the tradition and by new interpretations. In these two ways it makes sense to talk of an organic continuum, or the continuing life of dead artists, and this discovery of cultural immortality has often led to a sudden personal insight. We have already seen the testimony of Filarete and Alberti, but there are present-day versions where an artist simultaneously discovers the past and his contemporaries' relation to it. Evidence can be gathered from all quarters – not just from those 'revivalist' born-again classicists, in whose impassioned words the sudden inspiration is most evident, but also from committed 'survivalists', defenders of the faith whose ideals have not diminished even in the Modern epoch.

The art historian E H Gombrich has attempted to formulate a creed for such survivors as himself, heirs to the Western tradition. He acknowledges the way in which 'The Tradition of General Knowledge' is more an ideal than a current reality: the actual continuum of events, the number of significant individuals who make up its history, are much too large to be

intends and includes. If one were to modify it, as he asks, the most obvious additions would be at the beginning and end – Egyptian culture and the Modernist 'experiment' are the two most surprising lacunae.

There have been several times when the idea of a continuum has been expressed in art, notably during periods of revivalism when a strong historical consciousness is crossed with a sense of imminent creativity. Raphael's *School of Athens,* the *locus classicus* of classicism, is the best-known version of this reversible history.[5] Here the present and past are interwoven pictorially and symbolically as if all time were present at a single moment. This collapse of space and time represents in an immediate way the continuity of traditions, the past alive in the present and the present reanimating the past.

In architecture a similar idea is expressed by Gilbert Scott's Albert Memorial in London (4). Here Western culture is seen as a hierarchical evolution and the representation mixes a view of quality and worth with a more neutral historical narrative so that one writer leads to another, one artist to the next, both polemically and logically, both in terms of judgement and canonic history. Here a certain optimism places Shakespeare

4 SIR GEORGE GILBERT SCOTT, ALBERT MEMORIAL, LONDON, 1862-75: THE CONTINUUM OF WESTERN CULTURE

known, even by the specialist in cultural history. So another attack is called for, that adopted by the Church:

The classical tradition was only kept alive throughout the Dark Ages because a few learned churchmen such as Isidore of Seville were not ashamed of writing simple compendia to which they committed those few ideas about the universe and about the past which they considered indispensable, '. . . I have been toying with the idea of secular creeds, as brief and concise, if we can hammer them out, as the Athanasian Creed . . . It is with some trepidation that I submit for your criticism the first untidy draft of such a creed . . .

I belong to Western civilisation, born in Greece in the first millenium BC. It was created by poets, philosophers, artists, historians and scientists who freely examined the earlier myths and traditions of the ancient Orient. It flourished in Athens in the 5th century, was carried East by Macedonian conquests in the 4th century . . .'[4]

And there follows a concise history of the transformation of the classical tradition, 'biased, subjective and selective' as Gombrich is at pains to emphasise, but also cogent for what it

next to Homer and, on another panel, current architects next to their more renowned predecessors. This challenge thrown down to the past by the present typifies the hubris of contemporary culture, and is a direct consequence of regarding the past and present as a whole. After all, if both are part of the same continuum then the 'Moderns' can summarise and transcend the 'Ancients' in both quality and technical skill, as long as these aspects are narrowly defined.

Whatever goes into our collective view of Western culture as a living continuum, the very idea of it has key relevance for our subject. In so far as classicism is alive today it entails disputed interpretations and differing values. The subversive work of Robert Longo, for instance, while outside the canonic definition is nevertheless a part of the wider tradition in its appropriation of Roman forms for contemporary myths – to show what life is like in the large corporation (5). The protagonists of current classicism are no more likely to agree on every article of faith than are politicians as to the essence of democracy. In fact this debate, essential to the health of classicism, springs from ethical positions which are as fundamental as political and social ones. Any living tradition must challenge its roots, especially when

25

they are so venerable, and this leads to continuous reassessment and debate.

The New Rules

The new mode is provocative because it is both strange and yet very familiar. It combines two purist styles – canonic classicism and Modernism – and adds neologisms based on new technologies and social usage. Previous rules of decorum and composition are not so much disregarded, as extended and distorted. Indeed, the very notion of designing within a set of rules, which has been anathema since the Romantic age, takes on new meanings.

Now, rules or canons for production are seen as preconditions for creativity, a situation caused partly by the advent of the computer, which makes us conscious of the assumptions behind a building. Analytical scholarship within the art world has also increased this consciousness, as students are now forced to become aware of the conventions behind such seemingly spontaneous 20th-century movements as Primitivism and Expressionism. The only escape from rule-governed art is to suppress from consciousness the canons behind one's creativity

apparent in such popular films as *The Gods Must Be Crazy*, which alternates frequently betwen the world-view of a scientist, drop-out journalist, Kalahari Bushman and a revolutionist, yet manages to create from these a coherent drama. Significantly it appeals to different tastes and ages.

'Disharmonious harmony' also finds validity in the present consensus among scientists that the universe is dynamic and evolving. In the past, classical revivals have been associated with a presumed cosmic harmony. Vitruvius equated the 'perfect' human body with the celestial order and then justified the perfected order of the temple on these assumptions. The Renaissance, with its well-proportioned buildings and sculpture, followed these equations between microcosm and macrocosm. Today, however, with our compound and fragmented view of a Newtonian/Einsteinian universe, we have several theories of the macrocosm competing for our acceptance, none of which sound wholly plausible, complete or harmonious. Any scientist who has listened to the supposed origin of the universe – the noise of the Big Bang that apparently is still reverberating – does not speak only of 'the music of the spheres'; the 'violent universe' is as good a description of exploding supernovae as the

CHARLES JENCKS

5 ROBERT LONGO, *CORPORATE WARS: WALL OF INFLUENCE*, 1982, CAST ALUMINIUM; 6 STIRLING & WILFORD, CLORE GALLERY, ADDITION TO TATE, LONDON, 1982-6

– hardly a comforting liberation. And it's practically impossible to remain ignorant of these, at least of antecedent ones, in an age of constant communication and theorising. Thus, consciousness of rules and the irony which attends this, is thrust upon us. The following are the most significant of these emergent precepts:

1 The most obvious new convention concerns beauty and composition. In place of Renaissance harmony and Modernist integration is the new hybrid of *dissonant beauty,* or *disharmonious harmony.* Instead of a perfectly finished totality 'where no part can be added or subtracted except for the worse' (Alberti), we find the 'difficult whole' (Venturi) (7) or the 'fragmented unity' of architects like Hans Hollein (8) and artists like the Poiriers (13). This new emphasis on complexity and richness parallels the Mannerist emphasis on *difficultà* and skill, but it has a new social and metaphysical basis. From a pluralist society a new sensibility is formed which finds an oversimple harmony either false or unchallenging. Instead, the juxtaposition of tastes and world views is appreciated as being more real than the integrated languages of both exclusionist classicism and high Modernism. The new taste for disjunctions and collisions is

eternally ordered and calm picture behind classical and Christian art of the past.

Inevitably architecture and art must represent this paradoxical view, the oxymoron of 'disharmonious harmony', and it is therefore not surprising that we find countless formal paradoxes in Post-Modern work such as 'asymmetrical symmetry', 'syncopated proportion', 'fragmented purity', 'unfinished whole' and 'dissonant unity'. Oxymoron, or quick paradox, is itself a typical post-Modern trope and 'disharmonious harmony' recurs as often in its poetics as 'organic whole' recurs in the aesthetics of classicism and Modernism. The Japanese architect Monta Mozuna is characteristic of many architects in combining fragments of previous metaphysical systems into his buildings: Buddist, Hindu, Shinto and Western (9) . My own attempts at cosmic symbolism, realised in collaboration with the painter William Stok, mix 20th-century cosmology – the Big Bang theory, the concept of evolving galaxies and nebulae – with traditional views of morality and the idea of a cultural continuum. The heavens are traditionally represented by circles and spirals, the earth by squares or rectangles, and here this symbolism is reused on the ceiling (*coelum*) and floor (*terra*).

As strong a rule as 'disharmonious harmony', and one which justifies it, is *pluralism*, both cultural and political. The fundamental position of Post-Modernism in the 1970s was its stylistic variety, its celebration of difference, 'otherness' and irreducible heterogeneity. Feminist art and advocacy planning were two typical unrelated movements which helped form the tolerance of, and taste for, variety. In architecture, the stylistic counterpart of pluralism is *radical eclecticism* – the mixing of different languages to engage different taste cultures and define different functions according to their appropriate mood.

James Stirling's addition to the Tate Gallery is undoubtedly his most divergent creation to date, a building which changes surface as it meets different buildings and defines different uses (5). Where it attaches to the classical gallery it continues the cornice line and some of the stonework, but where it approaches a preexisting brick structure it adopts some of this red and white grammar. Its main entrance is different again, a formal grid of green mullioned glass which reappears in another main public area, the reading room. As if these changes were not enough to articulate the changing functions and mood, the grammar becomes Late-Modern to the rear – a style suitable to the service

tional role – the idea that an eclectic language speaks to a wide and divergent audience – something of a necessity for a public art gallery.

Enigmatic allegory and suggestive narrative are two Post-Modern genres which try to make a virtue of ambiguity and in this sense reflect an open, plural metaphysics. When several possible readings are presented simultaneously, it is left to the reader to supply the unifying text. This also entails frustration – the Post-Modern counterpart to the classical canon of 'withheld gratification'. Stirling's work is frustrating in the sense that it avoids a hierarchy of meanings. One has to look elsewhere to find a clearer expression of a unified view.

3 The most commonly held aim of Post-Modern architects is to achieve an *urbane urbanism:* the notion of contextualism has near universal assent. New buildings, according to this doctine, should both fit into and extend the urban context; reuse such constants as the street, arcade and piazza, yet also acknowledge the new technologies and means of transport. This double injunction amounts to a new rule, as clear and well defined as any tenet of canonic classicism. Furthermore, there are those

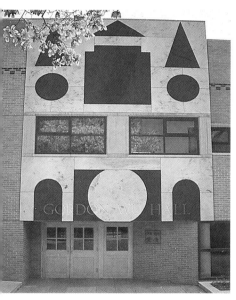 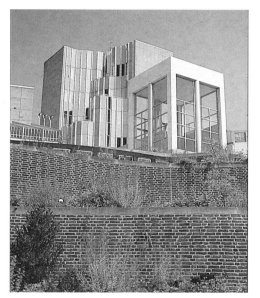 

VENTURI, RAUCH, SCOTT BROWN, GORDON WU HALL, 1982-4; 8 HOLLEIN, STADTISCHES MUSEUM, MONCHENGLADBACH, 1976-82; 9 MOZUNA, KUSHIRO CITY MUSEUM, 1982-4

area – and more neutral on the other side so as to be in keeping with the back of the Tate. To pull this heterogeneity together is a grid frame, presented as something analogous to a classical order. A square wall pattern, like the Renaissance application of pilasters, reappears again and again, inside and outside, to form the conceptual ordering system. But it is used in a dissonant not harmonious way – broken into quarter rhythms around the entrance, hanging in fragments over the reading room, and marching down part of the side facades. Thus Renaissance harmony is mixed with Modernist collage even in the background structure that is supposed to unify the fragments. While such extreme eclecticism may be questioned for such a small building, it does serve to characterise the heterogeneous functions, such as accommodating groups of schoolchildren, for which this building was specifically designed. Stirling speaks of it as a garden building attached to a big house, and this helps explain the informality, the lily pond, trellis work and pergola. It also underscores why this eclecticism is radical: because, unlike weak eclecticism which is more a matter of whim, it is tied to very specific functions and symbolic intentions. Another motive for the heterogeneity is its communica-

such as Leon Krier who would argue for an optimum relationship between all the parts of a city, a well-scaled balance between essential elements: public to private, work to living, monument to infill, short blocks to city grid, foreground square to background housing. If one focuses on this balance, rather than any particular set of dualities, then one will achieve the urbane urbanism of the Roman *insulae*, or the traditional 18th-century European city, or 19th-century American village. Small-block, mixed-use planning thus amounts to an urban prototype for convivial living. In Krier's schemes the physical and functional hierarchies are clear. There's no ambiguity, irony or juxtaposition here, which is why they seem at once so powerful and nostalgic. The urbane way of life is simply better suited to social intercourse than is the dissociated and overcentralised city, as seen in the SOM scheme for Boston (11).

4 The Post-Modern trope of *anthropomorphism* recurs in much current architecture as a subliminal image. Almost all of the new classicists incorporate ornament and mouldings suggestive of the human body. Geoffrey Scott in the *Architecture of Humanism*, 1914, applauded classicism because it 'transcribed in stone the body's favourable states'. Its profiles, as Michelangelo emphasised, could resemble silhouettes of a face; its sculptural mass and chiaroscuro could echo the body's muscles. Such architecture humanises inanimate form as we naturally project our physiognomy and moods onto it. This empathetic response is most welcome on large housing estates, or in a context which is fundamentally alienating or over-built. Jeremy Dixon (10), Robert Krier, Hans Hollein, Cesar Pelli, Kazumasa Yamashita and Charles Moore among others have developed this anthropomorphism, just as Michael Graves and I have tried to make abstract representations of the face and body in our work (12). The explicitness of the image varies from the obvious caryatid, or herm, to the hidden figure and seems most successful when combining these extremes. At a large scale the figure is best incorporated with other motifs and meanings, so it is not overpowering: in the Thematic House, for instance, head, shoulders, arms, belt and legs are as much arches and windows as they are anatomical parts. The general rule favours a subliminal anthropomorphism, but promotes an explicitness in detail and ornament. In an age when architects and artists are often at a loss for legitimate subject matter, the human presence

narrative without a plot. Anamnesis is one of the oldest rhetorical tropes and today has become a goal in itself.

6 The well-publicised 'return to painting' of Post-Modernism has also been accompanied by a 'return to content', and this content is as diverse and divergent as a pluralist society. The Hirschorn Museum exhibition, *Content*, 1974-84, showed some of this variety – the subject matter extended from autobiography to high and popular culture, from social commentary to metaphysical speculation, from paintings of nature to portrayals of psychological nature. In addition there was the extension of the traditional genres, such as narrative painting, still-life and landscape painting, summarised in exhibitions on realism.[7] There is clearly no underlying thread, coherence, mythology or emergent rule in this heterogeneity beyond the general 'will to meaning' as it was termed by the curator of the Hirschorn exhibition. Yet, through pluralism, the overall movement has a *divergent signification* and allows multiple readings through the convention of enigmatic allegory. Many Post-Modern critics have emphasised intertextuality (the way several discontinuous texts combine to form their own meaning) as both a strategy and

10 JEREMY DIXON, ST MARK'S ROAD, LONDON, 1976-9; *11* SOM (ADRIAN SMITH), ROWES WHARF, BOSTON

remains a valid departure point.

5 Another credible subject is the historical continuum and the relation between the past and present. This has led to an outbreak of parody, nostalgia and pastiche – the lesser genres with which Post-Modernism is equated by its detractors – but has also resulted in *anamnesis*, or suggested recollection. In a post-Freudian age the unconscious is often invoked as the source of anamnesis, and it works characteristically with the juxtaposition of related and opposed fragments. Ann and Patrick Poirier have captured this logic of dreams in their fragmented constructions which combine archetypes, half-remembered myths and miniature landscapes (13). We search these ruins for possible relations between such things as an arrow, bronze leaves and black lips; not fully comprehending the ancient story of which they may be fragments, but nevertheless invited to make a guess as to their significance. The enigmatic allegory makes use of dissociated and partial memories and, at best, creates a simulacrum of meaning where the overtones combine and harmonise. It is this harmonious aura which becomes the subject matter of this paradoxical genre – a

contemporary reality. This has led to two precepts, *radical eclecticism* in architecture and *suggestive narrative* in art.

7 The most prevalent aspect of Post-Modernism is its *double-coding*, use of irony, ambiguity and contradiction. Irony and ambiguity were key concepts in Modern literature and Post-Modernists have continued using these tropes and methods while extending them to painting and architecture. The idea of double-meaning and the *coincidentia oppositorum* ultimately goes back to Heraclitus and Nicholas of Cusa. Well before Robert Venturi and Matthias Ungers were formulating their poetics of dualism, a character in a Strindberg play exhorts 'Don't say "either . . . or" but instead "both . . . and"!'[8]

This Hegelian injunction has become *the* method for urban infill and is practised as a delicate art by Charles Vandenhove who stitches several parts of Belgian cities together with fragments of opposite languages. He has renovated the Hors-Chateau quarter of Liège with a variable order which has the dualism new/old consciously built in as a sign of reconciliation (14). His renovation of the Hotel Torrentius, a 16th-century mansion in the same city, is an exquisite compilation of opposites susceptible to several simultaneous readings: as real archaeological fragment, Secessionist ornament and as the superimposition of abstract geometries (16). The ironies and juxtapositions are underplayed in favour of a 'both/and' harmony. This attitude to the past, more like Renaissance mixing than Modernist collage, implies the historical continuum which is so essential to the Post-Modern vision. Present style and technology are accepted as valid realities, but not required to overassert themselves; it is a case of peaceful, not antagonistic, coexistence.

When Vandenhove adds a new facade to a museum of decorative arts, he invents a new stylised Ionic order, with oversized volutes made from concentric circles, but reconciles this with the previous geometry in a way that implies both continuity with the past and the separate identity of the present (15). This form of double-coding allows us to read the present in the past as much as the past in the present, as if history proceeded by a gradual evolution of permanent forms rather than a succession of revolutionary styles each one of which obliterates its predecessor. Double-coding can, of course, be used in an opposite way to emphasise the disjunctions, as for instance Stirling and Salle employ it; but however the method is articulated it acknowledges the simultaneous validity of opposite approaches.

8 When several codes are used coherently to some purpose they produce another quality sought by Post-Modernists, *multivalence*. A univalent building or Minimalist work of art can have integrity but only of an exclusive and generally self-referential type . By contrast, a multivalent work reaches out to the rest of the environment, to many adjacent references, and to many different associations. It is inclusive by intent and, when successful, resonant as a symbol. The resonance consists in linking forms, colours and themes. This idea – an old one stemming from the notion of 'organic unity' – is relatively rare in our culture where art and architecture have tended to go their separate ways: art to the gallery, and architecture to a limited institutional practice. Recently there have been many calls for collaboration, mutual commissions have been promoted, joint organisations formed; but most of these efforts have produced a juxtaposition of the two disciplines, rarely an integration of the art work and its setting.[9] Nevertheless, artists such as Eduardo

Paolozzi and Robert Graham, and architects such as Michael Graves and Cesar Pelli have sought a deeper collaboration that starts near the beginning of design, so that their work can be modified as it progresses. For mutual modification is the key to multivalence: only where the diverse meanings have been worked through will the art, architecture and daily activity begin to interact and form a greater unity.

Frank Lloyd Wright sought this organic unity in his work as did the Art Nouveau designers committed to the *Gesamtkunstwerk*. Churches often have a deliberate symbolic and aesthetic programme, but this is relatively rare in other building types. The great advantage and delight of multivalence is the continual reinterpretation it prompts, a result of the multiple links between the work and its setting. This unlimited semiosis (the continual discovery of new meaning in works that are rich in external and internal associations) is characteristic of both Post-Modernism and inclusive art in general. In Allen Jones' *Dance to the Music of Time*, 1984, for instance, one sees traditional representations of time (the Egyptian corn god, the Four Seasons, Father Time, youth etc) alongside more up-to-date ways of depicting the theme (such as the abyss of time dividing the aged musician from the exhibitionist dancer etc). If a work is resonant enough it continues to inspire unlimited readings.

9 A precondition for this resonance is a complex relation to the past: without memories and associations a building is diminished in meaning, while if it is purely revivalist its scope will be equally restricted. Hence the Post-Modern emphasis on anamnesis, or the historical continuum, and another of its defining rules – the displacement of conventions, or *tradition reinterpreted*. Most discussions of Post-Modernism focus on one or other of the many 'returns': the 'return to painting', figuration, ornament, monument, comfort, the human body and so on. The list is virtually endless, but all these returns must to some degree be inventive in order to transcend replication. Terry Farrell, for instance, will reinterpret the syntax and colour of the traditional temple form and use it on a boathouse in Henley (17). The festive polychromy of the Henley Regatta obviously forms the pretext for the strong blues and reds which also relate to the colours of the site and, incidentally, to 19th-century investigations into Greek polychromy. The temple columns become paired pilasters, the broken-pediment is extended down into the

12 MICHAEL GRAVES, PLOCEK HOUSE, NEW JERSEY, 1978-82; *13* ANN & PATRICK POIRIER, *UNTITLED*, 1984, BRONZE & MARBLE

brick base to become a water gate for the boats, and the acroteria become spot lights. The Henley blue is also an obvious sign of both water and sky, as is the waving ornament etched in the stucco frieze. Thus in many ways old forms are given new meanings to justify their existence. The proportions and flatness of detail, not to mention the saturated polychromy, appear strange at first glance (as do all such displacements of tradition) and it is only after we understand their new validity and they become familiar that the aura of pastiche disappears. The reinterpretation of tradition must always carry some overtones of this kind, since conventions are simultaneously affirmed and distorted.

10 Another way of renewing past conventions is by consciously elaborating *new rhetorical figures*. Post-Modernists, like the Modernists before them, or for that matter any historical movement, are definable by stylistic formulae which they invent or adapt. Fashion and function both play a role in establishing these new figures and the most prevalent are the ones we have touched on here: paradox, oxymoron, ambiguity, double-coding, disharmonious harmony, amplification, complexity and

are symptomatic of the taste for unfinished figures, incomplete classical shapes, and formality that is also informal. Marking a return to humanism, but without the full and confident metaphysics which supported it in the Renaissance, these erosions relate also to that feeling of loss which is a recurrent theme within Post-Modernism: the 'presence of the absence', such as the void in the centre of the Tsukuba Civic Centre (19).

11 This *return to the absent centre* is one of the most recurrent figures of Post-Modernism. It is portrayed both consciously by Arata Isozaki as a comment on the decentred nature of Japanese life, and unselfconsciously by James Stirling at Stuttgart, Michael Graves at the Humana Building, Ricardo Bofill at Montpellier and just about every Post-Modern architect who makes a central plan and then doesn't know what to put in the honorific place. This paradox is both startling and revealing: a desire for a communal space, a perfectly valid celebration of what we have in common, and then the admission that there is nothing quite adequate to fill it.

Perhaps this reflects the sense of loss which underlies so many of the departures which can be characterised with the prefix

CHARLES VANDENHOVE: *14* HORS CHATEAU, LIÈGE, 1978-86; *15* MUSEUM OF DECORATIVE ARTS, GHENT, 1986; *16* HOTEL TORRENTIUS, LIEGE, 1981-2

contradiction, irony, eclectic quotation, anamnesis, anastrophe, chiasmus, ellipsis, elision and erosion. Charles Moore has used the last three rhetorical devices recently to create something of a personal style. Characteristically he will erode a classical arch, or set of them, to create an ambiguous, layered space equivalent to the Baroque. But whereas these traditional forms were built in substantial masonry, Moore constructs them in plywood and stucco because it is both cheaper and lighter. Inevitably this is censored by some critics as scenographic architecture which deteriorates quickly, but the positive aspects of this innovation must not be overlooked. 'Cardboard architecture' allows new spatial experiences, new ways of joining thin surfaces which elide different shapes to create the effect of a run-on sentence, or a homogeneous and continuous structure. In the Sammis Hall (18), for instance, cut-out arches are held above by keystones, and on the sides by eroded Venetian windows, to form a magical, diaphanous space through which light pours and bounces. The complex ambiguity and layering are reminiscent of Vittone's Baroque domes, but the airy insubstantiality is very much of our time. Aside from economic motives, there is a psychological reason for the prevalence of such erosions – they

'post'. For, if we return to the first usage of the term by Arnold Toynbee and others in the 1940s and 1950s, we detect a similar melancholic connotation. Post-Modern then meant a culture that was post-Western and post-Christian; a culture that had a strong sense of its departure point, but no clear sense of destination. This ambivalence is worth stressing because, of course, the term also meant still-Modern and still-Christian – suggesting a very clear appreciation of the cultural roots and values embedded in everyday behaviour, law and language, which cannot disappear in one, two, or even five generations. The same is true of other global uses of the term – post-industrial and post-Marxist – they point as much to the very real survivals of preexisting patterns as they do to the transcendence of them. A post-industrial society, for instance, still depends fundamentally on industry no matter how much its power structure and economy have moved on to the next level of organisation – computers, information exchange and a service economy. The ambivalence accurately reflects this double state of transition, where activity moves away from a well known point, acknowledges the move and yet keeps a view, or trace, or love of that past location. Sometimes it idealises the security of this point of departure, with nostalgia and melancholy, but at the same time it may exult in a new-found freedom and sense of adventure. Post-Modernism is in this sense schizophrenic about the past; equally as determined to retain and preserve aspects of the past as it is to go forward; excited about revival, yet wanting to escape the dead formulae of the past. Fundamentally it mixes the optimism of Renaissance revival with that of the Futurists, but is pessimistic about finding any certain salvation point, be it technology, a classless society, a meritocracy or rational organisation of a world economy (ie, any of the answers which have momentarily been offered in the last 100 years). The 'grand narratives', as Jean-François Lyotard insists, have lost their certainty even if they remain locally desirable. The mood on board the ship of Post-Modernism is that of an Italian and Spanish crew looking for India, which may, if it's lucky, accidentally discover America; a crew which necessarily transports its cultural baggage and occasionally gets homesick, but one that is quite excited by the sense of liberation and the promise of discoveries.

There are more generative values in Post-Modern architecture

tradition of humanism. The modern world, which started with the Renaissance as an economic, social and political reality, has itself integrated as a 24-hour market-place on a much more complex level. Modern communications, scholarship and fabrication methods make any and every style equally possible, if not equally plausible. Even more than in the 19th century, the age of eclecticism, we have the freedom to choose and perfect our conventions and this choice forces us to look both inwards and outwards to culture as a whole. For the Modernist predicament, often epitomised in Yeats' words – 'Things fall apart; the centre cannot hold' – we have the dialectical answer – 'Things fall together, and there is no centre, but connections'. Or in E M Forster's words – 'connect, only connect'.

Notes

1 *Antonio Filarete, Traktat über die Baukunst,* (ed) W Von Oettingen, Vienna, 1890, IX, p 291. Quoted and translated by Erwin Panofsky, *Renaissance and Renascences in Western Art*, 1960; taken from the Paladin Edition, Granada, London, 1970, pp 19-20.
2 L B Alberti, *Della Pittura*, Florence, 1435, preface. Quoted from Michael Greenhalgh, *The Classical Tradition in Art*, Harper and Row, London and

17 TERRY FARRELL, HENLEY BOAT HOUSE, 1984-6; *18* MOORE GROVER HARPER, SUMMIS HALL, COLD SPRING HARBOUR; *19* ARATA ISOZAKI, TSUKUBA CIVIC CENTRE, 1981-3

and art than these 11 formulae and they are, inevitably, in a state of evolution. Furthermore, like the values and motives of any large movement, they are partly inconsistent. Nevertheless, these emerging canons are, in the third, classical phase of Post-Modernism, beginning to develop a discernible shape and direction, and we can say that this year's version of the ornamental building is likely to be more sophisticated than last year's. Urban building codes are evolving in a more enlightened direction as client and architect become more aware of the importance of context, while the many 'returns' in art have, in limited ways, made it richer and more accessible. Rules, however, do not necessarily a masterpiece make, and tend to generate new sets of dead-ends, imbalances and urban problems. Hence the ambivalence of our age to orthodoxy and the romantic impulse to challenge all canons of art and architecture while, at the same time, retaining them as a necessary precondition for creation: simultaneously promoting rules and breaking them. We are still near the beginning of the classical phase, which started in the late 1970s, and although one cannot predict its future, it is likely to deepen as it synthesises the distant and more recent past, as it sustains more profoundly the Western

New York, 1978, p 80.
3 T S Eliot, 'Tradition and the Individual Talent', *Sacred Wood*, Methuen & Co, London, 1920, pp 49-50.
4 E H Gombrich, 'The Tradition of General Knowledge', *Ideas and Idols*, Phaidon, Oxford, 1979, pp 21-2.
5 For the idea that Raphael's *School of Athens* epitomises the classical tradition and for a discussion see Michael Greenhalgh, *op cit*, pp 15-17.
6 *Content, A Contemporary Focus*, 1974-84, Hirschorn Museum, Washington DC, 4-6 Jan 1985; curated by Howard N Fox; essays by Fox, Miranda McClintic and Phyllis Rosenzweig.
7 For these categories and the best discussion of realist painting today see Frank H Goodyear Jr *Contemporary American Realism Since 1960*, exhibition catalogue and book, New York Graphic Society, Boston, 1981.
8 Strindberg's dualism is discussed in James McFarlane's 'The Mind of Modernism', *Modernism 1890-1930*, (eds) Malcolm Bradbury and James McFarlane, Penguin Books, Harmondsworth, 1976; quote from p 88.
9 For the recent conferences, exhibitions and commissions involving the collaboration between artists and architects see *Collaboration*, (ed) Barbara Lee Diamonstein, Architectural Press, London.

An earlier version of this article appeared in Charles Jencks' Post-Modernism – The New Classicism in Art and Architecture, *Academy Editions, London/Rizzoli, New-York*

JOSE-IGNACIO LINAZOSORO
Reconstruction of a Church
Medina de Rioseco

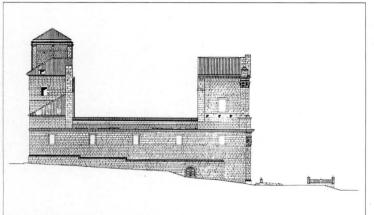
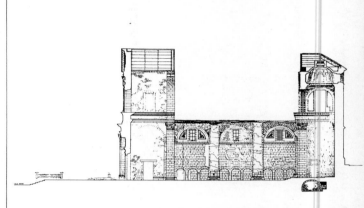
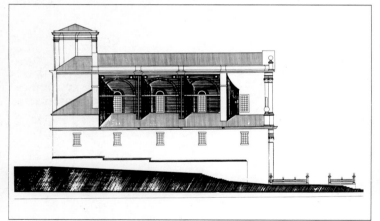
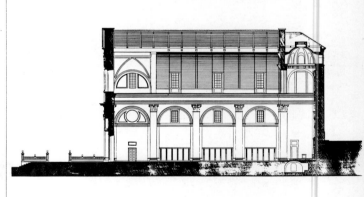

SOUTHEAST ELEVATION AND LONGITUDINAL SECTIONS. *ABOVE*: REMAINING STRUCTURE; *BELOW*: RECONSTRUCTION

Before it fell into ruin, the central nave of the Sacred Heart church had been covered with a massive coffered vault supported by thick buttresses. The problem in restoring it was that the walls – from the cornice line of the lower Order up – seemed in no condition to support such a heavy structure. It was imperative to find an alternative, light material that would still be in keeping, both compositionally and spatially, with the building as a whole. Replicating the Baroque decoration of the vault did not seem important, as this had been completed some time after the rest of the church, and expressed as much by its resolutely different character. A more purely architectural ornament was needed to establish a dialogue with the figurative image of the church. The solution was to use timber, which was both capable of repeating the vaulted forms and light enough to ensure the stability of the building.

In rebuilding the upper portion of the exterior, brick load-bearing arches were used in place of the original massive walls. These not only prevented overloading but also created a formal roundness which provided the starting point for a compositional revision of the side elevations. Previously, the sides had been very much subordinate to the main facade. Now, through the open expression of the brickwork in the reconstructed section, and the addition of a parapet, a more unified and complete treatment is achieved.

The interior of the church used to be cluttered with reredos and heavy pieces of furniture. Leaving the church bare after restoration, however, would have deprived it of all those references which convey a sense of proportion, so a few items of modern furniture were carefully chosen to enhance the clean, architectural lines of the space.

Jose-Ignacio Linazosoro

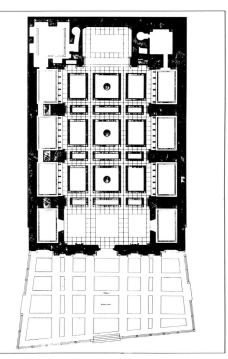

ABOVE AND CENTRE: DETAILS OF RECONSTRUCTION WORK; *BELOW*: NEW AND OLD CEILING VAULT, GROUND PLAN

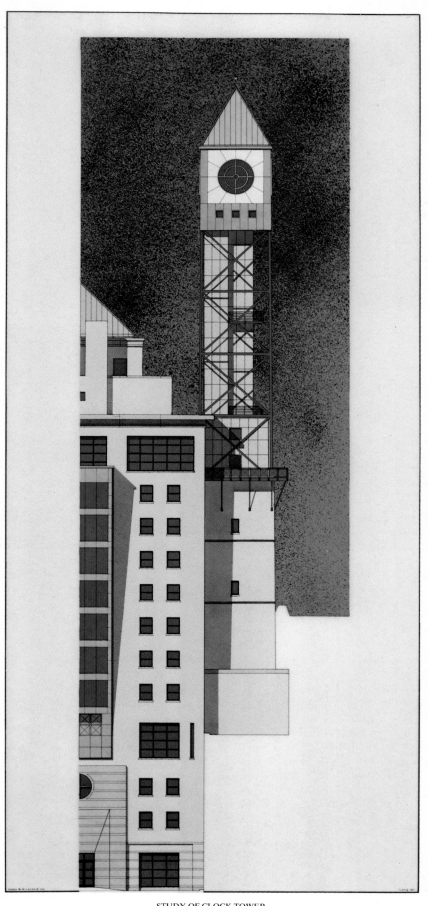

STUDY OF CLOCK TOWER

JONES & KIRKLAND
Mississauga City Hall
With a Critique by Robert Maxwell

VIEW OF FACADE BUILDING AND CIVIC SQUARE

The competition for the new City Hall at Mississauga presented the challenge of creating a piece of civic architecture for an, as yet, featureless urban landscape. The initial sketches were made before the competition conditions were known and tackled the problem of making a 'somewhere of a nowhere location'. Some of these early architectural 'notes' were referential, looking at the concept of a city hall as a memory of the city in miniature, contained within its own internal

ogic, indifferent to its surroundings and using many elements of Asplund's Nordic classicism. The brief, which was finally circulated in June 1982, gave an intelligent, highly detailed framework for the building and its urban design environment. The programme was for a building of 40,000 square metres on a site 19,500 square metres in area, lying adjacent to a large regional shopping centre, itself set within a superblock ringed by 12-storey office towers, the ground between covered by parking lots.

The site of the new city hall is on the divide between town and country and the architects explored the possibility of combining the two related architectural traditions: the strong 19th-century urban tradition of Greater Toronto with tree-lined residential streets and monumental, honorific public architecture, and the vigorous, functional agrarian architecture of barns, grain silos and water towers whose solids recalled memories of classical civic ensembles. The historical use of a grand scale, a Beaux-Arts composition and durable materials clearly distinguished the civic from private buildings, providing landmarks and a public infrastructure, unlike the more recent, supposedly egalitarian, avoidance of issues of metaphor, hierarchy and the associative power of forms.

Jones and Kirkland have returned to these issues in a building that is recognisably civic. Two possible schemes were developed; one distributed the building around three sides of the square, this maintained the continuity of the street surface, but was later rejected for its introspection, organisational and energy problems, it was also felt that the southern European square was

antipathetic to the harsh Canadian winters and the historical Ontario model. The preferred organisational scheme was for a consolidated building on the northern edge of a square completed by freestanding arcades and gardens. This plan allowed more convenient conections between departments and a greater richness of interior section and public spaces. The idea was developed of a 'building for two seasons', the square as public room in summer, the lobby its internal equivalent in winter.

The building stands on a plinth five foot above ground to distinguish it from the surrounding area. The principal facade forms a civic foreground and acts as mediator between outdoor civic square and indoor city hall, each with their equivalent and complementary spaces. Behind the facade are grouped a number of principal programme elements. In front of the facade these are complemented and contrasted by the amphitheatre with its references to European classicism and the public gardens which look west to the prairies.

Partners in Charge: Edward Jones, Michael Kirkland; *Project Architects:* Steve Teeple, Maxim James, Gerry Lang, Kit Wallace, Mark Sterling; *Project Administrators:* Bernard Gillespie, Endel Arro, Matt Poray, Jack Shaw; *Project Team:* Marc Baraness, James Brown, Sydney Browne; Donna Clare, Margot Griffin, Michael Griffin, Courtney Henry, Hong Kim, Jeff Latto, Dan McNeil, Ian Moore, Neil Morfitt, Sarah Pearce, Jose Pereira, Suzanne Powadiuk, George Przybylski, Chris Radigan, Val Rynnimeri, Terry Shimbashi, Jon Soules, Kim Stoery; *Consultants:* M S Yolles, Structural, T M P, Mechanical, Mulvey & Banani, Electrical; *Construction Managers:* The Jackson-Lewis Company Ltd; *Client:* City of Mississauga.

All photographs, unless otherwise credited, are by Robert Burley Photography

L TO R: VIEW FROM SOUTHWEST; VIEW FROM SOUTHEAST

L TO R: VIEW FROM NORTHEAST; VIEW OF CITY HALL FROM SOUTHEAST

MISSISSAUGA IS SAID TO BE A SUBURB OF Toronto, but this description is misleading. It is an adjacent centre of growth. Heading west out of Toronto in the direction of Mississauga is very much like heading west out of Dallas in the direction of the 'twin' city of Fort Worth. There, it's far from obvious at what point you've finally reached your destination, because of the erratic impact of development along the way; here also, in an urban landscape dominated by spreading factory sheds along with the urban paraphernalia of drive-in banks, motels and gas stations, the eye searches for a landmark, for something of significance to latch on to. Indeed, the horizon is interrupted at irregular intervals by large lumps of building, all vaguely impressive, even sacramental – like gaunt cathedrals of the 20th century – until on closer approach they identify themselves all too clearly as industrial installations, or more mundanely, as hotels or office blocks. Eventually, a closer grouping of office blocks on adjacent sites takes on the semblance of a miniature downtown – a downtown that is coming rather than going. Then, soon after, another problematic mass, a tightly knit group that has something industrial, or agricultural, about it; but also a touch of Bavarian monastery or Italian hill town.

This time, closer approach does not dissipate the mystery: this time, we are dealing with architecture, and we have reached the improbable hub of the future city of Mississauga.

As we approach, the massing resolves itself into two aspects: a forecourt flanked by colonnades that extend in front of a large pedimental mass, and a cluster of varied building forms behind it, on its north side. The forecourt is unmistakably formal, with its central pool and double rows of copper beeches. There is no doubt that the building 'faces' south; and in this it follows a local tradition, for to face south in Toronto means addressing not only the sun but the great lake and the world of business opportunities and cultural engagements that exists indefinitely on the far side of it. To the north lies the tundra.

If you work here and use the underground car park which lies beneath the plaza podium, you will ascend to ground level via one of the two terminal pavilions (one to each colonnade), and will then follow the colonnade to entrances which lead through lobbies to the Great Hall – the central space of the building. The central opening on the south facade, however, which gives directly into the winter garden, is reserved for rare and important ceremonial occasions. The winter garden, with its mossy

OPENING CEREMONY, 1987

columns and fluttering birds, speaks of a warmer clime and imparts a touch of fantasy, which impinges on the Great Hall as well. If you arrive by taxi or bus you'll be dropped off at a central point on the north front, entering the Great Hall towards the winter garden, towards the source of light. The juxtaposition of these two central spaces is important in creating a sense of place, for the winter garden, by screening the view out to the ceremonial plaza, prevents the building from emptying itself prematurely. It produces a density in the direction of the main axis to match the density of the cross axis. The cross axis could be said to balance the council chamber on the east with the office block on the west, albeit with some shifts of geometry, and with the introduction of other elements like the grand staircase and (higher up) the clock tower.

These complications are useful in modifying the symbolic meaning of the principal oppositions employed by the architects, which, all the same, work orthogonally around the biaxial focus in the Great Hall. The Great Hall mediates the building. It opposes the empty plaza with its ceremonial entrance screened by the fantastical garden, to the humdrum sidewalk entrance on the other side, with its constant stream of arrivals and departur-

es. It opposes the Council Chamber – an enclave of privilege and responsibility – to the office block, with its daily comings and goings. It thus takes on something of the quality of a city square, absorbing and neutralising the presences of the Commonwealth, of the City Government, of the Union of Workers, of the People. It reconstitutes a city within the city, compensating for the sub-urban sprawl outside by an architectural compaction within. But although the oppositions are more or less biaxial, they are not so obvious as to allow meaning to drain away at a glance. The Great Hall is cool, not hot. There is no exaggerated use of emblems, for instance, or of emblematic 'figures' on each face of the square. Yet there is no doubt that in adapting the ancient idea of axes, the architects have been thinking not just about the ordering of the spaces, but about their meaning, and about the representational nature of the vertical surfaces which define them. In a very definite way, this building is 'about' the representation of function. It is a serious attempt to make public architecture, to return architecture to a theatre of public life.

The Great Hall is a foursquare, four-storey-high space, surmounted by a pyramidal glazed roof. At ground level, the space expands behind colonnades on all four sides, but at the higher

L TO R: FACADE DETAIL FROM CIVIC SQUARE; AMPHITHEATRE

L TO R: EXTERNAL PASSAGEWAY; ARCADED CORRIDOR ROUND CIVIC SQUARE

levels, wall surfaces, punctured by small square windows, define the volume in the way a town square is defined by surrounding buildings. The columns and the upper wall surfaces are picked out in verde alpe marble from Carrara, with narrow bands in black Uruguayan granite. The floors are also covered with polished marble, pink squares of rosso verona, also banded in black granite. The effect is both lush and austere, certainly grand. It suggests something of the largesse which might be prompted by a good hotel, or the indulgence of a shopping mall, until one remembers that this is the seat of government – the theatre of politics, not of consumption. At the same time it represents the varied functions of a community centre that provides a great many services: advice on business development, an art gallery, a public fitness centre equipped with the latest muscle machines, a sauna, squash courts, a public restaurant, a centre for daycare services, a wedding chapel, a scenic garden, an outdoor amphitheatre, a sculpture court, a variety of venues for private and public functions and the water feature in the ceremonial court converts to an ice-rink in winter. The presence of all these activities is somehow spoken for in the interior facades of the Great Hall: looked at as a kind of

department store or shopping mall, it is on the austere side, but as the seat of government, it is an assertion of community and urban identity in the face of a formless and unfinished environment. One could say that promptings to consumption have been replaced for the time being by promptings to civic order, and that by evoking a theatre of action, the building poses in succinct form the question of democratic renewal which has been claimed for architecture in the Post-Modern era.

Strictly, it is the Council Chamber that is the theatre of government, and this impression is confirmed within it. In the circular space, the diameter divides the benches of the councillors from the seating reserved for the general public, and while the councillors are certainly treated as actors, and have a very good behind-the-scenes support system, they are not only on show, but accountable to their audience. The sense of theatre is reinforced by the paired Tuscan columns that define the edge and support the banded wall beneath the dome. At the time of my visit, a test had just been run on the acoustic performance of an opera singer in this space, with apparently promising results. It has indeed something of the intimacy and voluptuousness of a small opera house, complete with artistic decoration of the

THE GREAT HALL AND COUNCIL CHAMBER FROM THE ROOF TERRACE

dome itself – sky-blue to depict an evening sky over Mississauga, and studded with stars that twinkle by means of a miracle of fibre-optics, together with a portrayal of the Indian legend of the Great Bear and the Seven Hunters, which explains the changing of the seasons through the progression of a hunt. Remote as this legend may be from the realities of developmental politics, it has something of the calming effect of all mythical art: violence and death have been transformed into unearthly beauty, an encouragement to councillors and partisans alike that, one day, their dogfights may be ennobled.

Each principal space has been decorated so as to express its function in social terms that all can understand. The councillors' caucus room is a particularly good example: it repeats motifs similar to those found in the Council Chamber, but with wood rather than marble, so that the character turns towards club rather than theatre. The foyers outside the Council Chamber, where the members are lobbied, are comparatively undecorated, and become 'Modern'-looking by that very comparison, as if to express the informality appropriate to the activity of lobbying, and also to a space that is compositionally to be classed as *poche*. This is very skilful decoration, if that is what it

is. By a similar token, the staircase giving access to the various public offices is distinctly grander in conception and in finishes than the offices themselves, which are nonetheless decorated, albeit in simpler materials, with the same family of details used in the honorific parts of the building. The impression made by the staircase is due not only to its noble ancestry – *scale regia* genre – but to the calculated way in which its matt walls are enlivened by narrow bands of polished marble that reflect the light on down from the high skylight above. In this way economy in the use of marble becomes in itself a means of sensual enticement, and at the same time repeats the themes of the building, with its stone bandings and podium, reiterating the sense of identity; so that the building becomes at every level, inside and out, a representation of a primal meaning, a sort of people's palace.

The architects have worked to ensure that all parts of the building fall under a consistent rule of decoration. This has involved the design of special fittings, such as the dished wall lights. It has also involved a judicious choice of materials: the elevators, for example, are lined with stainless steel panels that match the standard doors. Some of the door fittings are standard

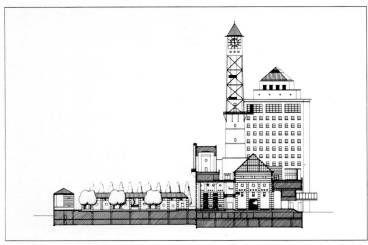
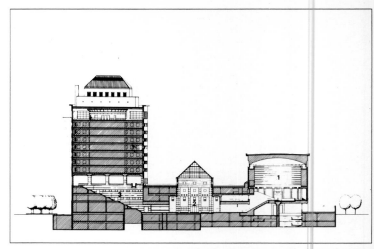
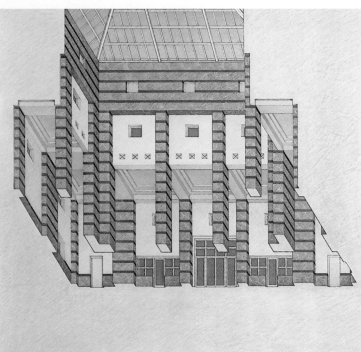

ABOVE L TO R: NORTH-SOUTH SECTION, EAST-WEST SECTION; *BELOW L TO R*: WORM'S EYE VIEW OF GREAT HALL; THE GREAT STAIR

off-the-peg items that were first marketed in the 1930s, and the prevailing atmosphere is indeed somewhat reminiscent of that period, without being exactly imitation Art Deco. The rule of consistency means that even the potted plants, which are ubiquitous, are always large, and always contained in the same jumbo earthenware pots.

It is refreshing, and unusual, to have so much engaging material in the interior of the building. It has been more usual for architects to 'save' their concept for the outside, and abandon the inside to its occupants. Part of this attention to detail must be due to the climate, which in this part of the world is severe enough in winter to make indoor living essential; indeed, the Civic Centre is billed in the official brochure under the architects' original competition title: 'A Building for Two Seasons'. Again, the identity of the Centre has been forcibly asserted against the suburban formlessness outside, as much as against threats of snow and ice, proclaiming an inner empire with every confidence that it will be taken up by the people (those that I talked with took evident pleasure in being in possession of a stylish building).

While this may mean no more than that everyone has been glad to move into a posh new facility, this building shows every indication of becoming a popular success. It has been designed to be made sense of, and it makes sense. The decoration of the interior seems to come over as something deserving respect. The architects clearly belong to a class of experts who know what they are about, like the special effects people of 'The Empire Strikes Back', or the producers of Sade's videos. Every part of the building has been taken into consideration, and has received its share (a 'proper' share) of the whole.

The outside of the building is equally explicit. The prominent cylindrical form of the Council Chamber clearly honours an institution, while carrying reminiscences of grain silo. The municipal offices are given the autonomy of an office block, with the culminating silhouette familiar from well-known examples standing free on their own sites in Canadian cities. The clock-tower is a clock tower, with suggestions of water tower. The pedimental mass is a front, with overtones of barn. The parts are not therefore enigmatic in themselves, but seem familiar, although somewhat unexpectedly associated together. That they belong together, however, seems not in doubt, since the same meticulous attention to materials and detail binds them

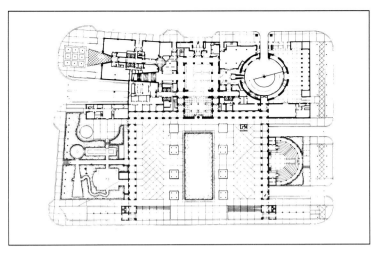

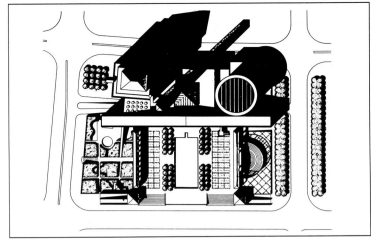

ABOVE L TO R: GROUND FLOOR PLAN, SITE PLAN OF INITIAL SCHEME; *BELOW:* THE GREAT HALL, INTERIOR VIEWS

together with the same loving care as the inside spaces. The bricks were imported from Pennsylvania, chosen not only for their colour, texture and large size, but for their freedom from problems of efflorescence. The 'stone' bandings are made of acid-etched pre-cast concrete, which looks exactly like limestone in context. The roofs are of copper, which will one day be a coppery shade of green, and the aluminium trim has been anodised this terminal shade in advance. This is a far cry from the too-easy simulation of fanciful images in plywood or stucco, which we have come to associate with the Post-Modern. The mode of building is substantial, intended to last, and it seems to be part of its acceptance by the community that the funds to build it were all raised in advance, so that the city is not in debt on account of this investment.

But if the building is perceived as amiable, and if it has succeeded in communicating some idealised sense of its purpose to its users, as it seems to have done, does this make it good architecture?

The critic must remain sceptical about this question. There have been many cases where a building has found acceptance in its time, and been rejected by a wider public. The sense of the satisfied user is part of a good situation that makes everybody concerned happy; responsibilities have been fulfilled, the architects are looking for another opportunity and another client. But the judgement of architecture seems to call for another kind of assessment. By this I do not mean the moral judgement that asks only one question: does this building serve society as it is? This judgement seems to collapse at once into a moral condemnation of the building along with the society that it manifestly serves: if the society is corrupt, how can the building be otherwise?

If the building finds a ready response in its public, this can only mean that it shares an ideological position with its public. In this case, the expectation that, through the operation of capitalist economics and the opportunities for profit that real estate development offers, the hinterland will grow as rapidly as possible so that the Civic Centre will really find itself the centre of a dense urban scene, at which point the wide expanse of its ceremonial plaza will take on a quite different value, just as will the cheek-by-jowl placement of the office block, reception wing and the Council Chamber. Clearly the building was designed in that expectation, and can only reach its fulfilment when those conditions have been realised. These conditions were explicit in

41

L TO R: CENTRAL COLUMN IN UNDERGROUND CAR PARK; MYTHOLOGICAL CEILING IN COUNCIL CHAMBER

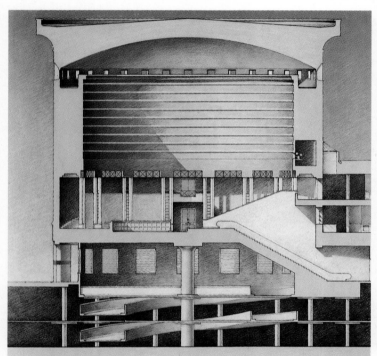

L TO R: SECTION THROUGH COUNCIL CHAMBER; ENTRANCE TO COUNCIL CHAMBER

the competition brief, prepared with the advice of George Baird, and several of the entries might have gained as much success as the winners in achieving its goals. To be able to decide if this is a case of good architecture, we need to turn to something beyond development policies, social acclaim, professional competence, ideological convenience. We need to refer to the condition of architecture, and ask how this building affects that.

There seems no doubt that the building has communicated a character, and that it has succeeded in this by means of a skilful rhetoric, making allusions not only to the familiar silhouettes of agricultural or city elements, but to a generation of buildings that were loved and accepted for their details, like 1930s cinemas and town halls. It is the density of allusions thrown off that enables people to place it into their conceptual maps, and so place themselves in it. But this play of allusions extends also into a less popular realm, where it engages with architectural theory. The division into separate elements, for instance, is a reaction against the packaging of buildings into a single bland box. Not only does this disaggregation reduce the scale, but it allows the architect to re-enter the field of composition, as has been ably demonstrated on many occasions by Leon Krier and his follow-

ers. It has been pointed out that the pedimental 'barn' at Mississauga could be derived from the pedimental gateway at the entry to Krier's project for a school at St Quentin-en-Yvelines. It also has a relation to the narrow *barre* building of many Constructivist and Neo-Constructivist compositions, with cells strung on a single corridor because they are all entitled, in a rational and egalitarian world, to the same orientation. More exactly, since such a form establishes a decisive front, it brings us back to the way Le Corbusier explored frontage zones as if they were canvases against which Cubist volumes could be placed in play; in front, as in the case of the Salvation Army Hostel in Paris, or above, as in the Unité at Marseilles. The play of office tower, clock tower and cylindrical tower above the barn-like silhouette of the pedimental block makes a clear reference to this idea of composition, and this is something more than simple character reference, in that it brings into consideration the means of assemblage, the very basis of abstract art.

Equally, one can concede that the cylindrical mass of the Council Chamber has more to do with Asplund, and Nordic classicism, than with grain silos, however convenient that association may be in this case. In a wider sense that interest is strong

COUNCIL CHAMBER, INTERIOR VIEW

today, as architects test their hold on classical antecedents by comparison with other societies for whom it was exotic. But the form also has a fascination because it is such a strong plan figure that it raises immediately the age-old question of *poche*, the means by which, outside of it, the architect can modulate back to the dominant orthogonal system of spaces. Here, as we have noticed, the *poche* space is given the positive value of a lobby – a place for lobbying – which makes it functionally useful, not just a lost zone for closets and service stairs. This is a highly significant trait, for it shows that the architects are in the business of trying to restore the *poche* as a useful principle of planning, allowing them to employ a hierarchical set of spaces without returning all the way to traditional plan making. A further instance of this occurs in the various uses made of the volumes immediately behind the pedimental wall. These are sometimes significant spaces, such as the Chief Planner's office, and sometimes not, suggesting an ambiguity as to whether this is a *barre* block or a frontage wall; that is, whether it acts as a separate spatial element or as a screen which relates to the composition as a whole. This ambiguity may be found throughout as a mode of questioning the space of decision which lies between abstraction and concretion, and which lies also between the use of forms that are known and bear meaning, and the syntactical mode of setting these forms together to generate new meanings.

It is not enough to characterise this architecture as contextualism, or regionalism, because to be contextual and regional is part of the duty laid on every architect who wants to do a good job. Clearly, an architecture limited only to making associational allusions ends up in Disney's empire. To be more, architecture has to place itself inside its own tradition and question the value *to architecture* of the discoveries of the day, such as abstraction (which we should perhaps refer to as 'abstraction'); and, in particular, to test the continuing validity of traditional modes of operation, above all composition.

It is the nature of these concerns which makes this building of particular interest to critical theory. It projects a point of view which is as antipathetic to Post-Modern kitsch as it is to negative dialectic and other forms of protest. The one reduces architecture to consumption, the other rejects architecture in order to reject consumption. Such judgements are satisfactory only to those who wish to remove architecture from its position as discourse.

CASA AURORA, VIEW OF CORNER, GROUND FLOOR PLAN AND FACADE DETAIL

ALDO ROSSI
Casa Aurora & Other Recent Projects

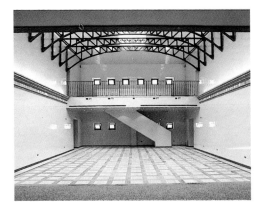

ABOVE: INTERIOR OF THEATRE, STREET ARCADE; *BELOW*: STREET ELEVATIONS

'Casa Aurora is a beautiful name, and as I believe in names that continue through time – like urban traces – it at once seemed a fortunate project. This Casa Aurora is, it seemed to me, a mysterious, almost mythological name. This often happens in toponymy, which is a discipline related to architecture: for example it has always struck me that in Turin one of the most important and beautiful streets – without doubt amongst the most beautiful in the world – has, in place of some grandiose name, always retained its true name, that of the street at the gate to the Po, as found in villages throughout the Po plain – Via Po.

I believe that this new Casa Aurora is connected also to the discovery of a most rational and complex Turin, and I have tried to express that at least as a fragment. Others have spoken of the architecture of this building: I can only say that I have sought to understand the city through her urban structure, both simple and ornate, and to understand her architecture, above all the grand public buildings designed by architects from Alfieri to Caselli through the work of the man who, to me, is the city's greatest architect, Alessandro Antonelli.

Often I understand buildings by looking at them like people; as if one can study destiny with clinical eyes. That's why I have also talked of fragments. As I see it, the new city will be composed of more and more diverse and significant parts, but these diverse fragments of a broken-up system will recompose in the unity we search. Turin, unlike most other Italian cities, such as Naples or Milan, was not a city of fragments; on the contrary, she was the united city *par excellence*. But today I believe that the whole centre, in this perfect system, must be considered like a precious part for reordering the design of the whole city.' *Aldo Rossi*

Casa Aurora, 1984-7, new building for Gruppo Finanzario Tessile.

45

ALDO ROSSI

Fragments

'The artist feels at times that his system, even if it is only practical or technical, becomes fragmented in his work. That each work is at once a "unicum", an entity, and a repetition.

It struck me that . . . fragments, their personal natures aside, could be seen to express the state of the modern city, of architecture, and of society.

In Italian *frammento*, fragment, means a small chip broken from a larger body. Following this definition fragments can be regarded as objects of hope; a multitude or accumulation of broken objects should not, therefore, be considered to amount to a scrap-heap. In this light, if changes are not effected, if disorder continues to be accepted, and if no thoughtful provisions are made, the scrap-heap may well turn out to be the city of the future instead.

Among the many other meanings of *frammenti*, fragment is the literary and artistic term used to describe the remains of a larger work. The fragments of a book, for instance, or the fragments that are the known works of a poet, the greater part of whose oeuvres have been lost. Whether given their physical definition (broken objects, detached elements) or general meaning (the surviving parts of a whole), fragments belong without doubt to the world of architecture. They belong as solid, built elements, and as theoretical elements. The first, being concrete, are more readily recognisable than the second, where fragments constitute the remains of a ruined general theory.

The ruins of an aqueduct or the chips of a sapphire can be seen more immediately as architecture than can fragments of antique, antiquated or modern, urban and social ideologies.

Physical fragments lead us to exclaim, as do the books about our heroes and books of fairy tales, "*cara architettura!*", "dear architecture!" In the final analysis, architecture's substance, genesis and relatively short life seem so human that we cannot help but regard it with affection.

When I look at each of my projects I believe I can still say, without being misleading, "Strange how like myself I am." The likeness appears in daily routine, in the love of objects fragmented or damaged, the impossible day-to-day demands of the profession, oppressive technicalities, the perfectioning of a system whereby all the fragments come together in the end. It is possibly this reuniting of fragments that is the realm of significance: we can reconstruct *ad absurdum* or expect a miracle, but we cannot accept it at a lower value.

Yet we who have always placed architecture among the arts and trades do not care to consider it on this level of values. A strange and simple sentiment makes us love our trade and I should like to repeat "*cara architettura!*"

This means that the most complex dissertations on ways of living "cannot keep the dog away from the warmth of the stove", it also represents a eulogy of civil architecture. I believe that there is plenty of room, between the two extremes of homely warmth of the stove and civil architecture, for that which we regard on a daily basis as "architecture". It is an "architecture" indifferent to the chattering traffic of associations, university chairs, periodicals and exhibitions.

These comments may appear to be a contraction of a broader discussion. It is useless, however, to search for fragments beyond this mass of remnants and broken pieces, for they are submerged in a multitude or accumulation of abandoned objects.

And what of my work? . . . I grow ever more involved in the constructions, rising as they do in places so dissimilar and occupying such a great part of my life. I believe I shall describe them one day, when I am old, when the longing for things has been utterly overcome by the desire to tell of them. It is difficult to

L TO R: DRAWING OF THE COURTYARD, DE AMICIS SCHOOL, BROMI; *LA CITTÀ VERTICALE*

46

predict when such a time will come . . .

Finally, on the subject of architecture, I still have a dream of great civil architecture; not the concordance of discord, but the city that is beautiful because of the wealth and variety it contains. I believe in the city of the future for this reason. It is a place where the fragments of something once broken are recomposed. In truth the recomposition does not seek a single, overall design but the liberty of a life of its own, a freedom of styles.

A city that is free.'   *Aldo Rossi*

rationalist and a romantic in his approach to architecture. His is the poetic classicism of understatement based on proportion. His forms have a unity and simplicity, they are contemporary yet look at tradition, derived from his concept of the city. Rossi has a distinctive personal style yet opposes the idea of the architect imposing his own private personality upon public architecture. His drawings emphasise his concept of fragmentation. Elements are taken from the Italian architectural tradition and from his own personal vocabulary; square windows, triangular elements, austere arcading, and conical towers are set in sketches against historical domes, but

gives them their individuality of character, related to socio-economic and political factors of past and present and to their particular topography. The architect must not impose alien materials of the International Style, but has to respond to what is there. The future is merged with the past, novelty with recollection. The man-made environment of the city is the materialisation of memory. Rossi recognises the wealth of the long Italian urban tradition. A new building reflects the historical memory, it establishes a relationship with existing structures to give a fresh meaning to the city. This can be seen at Casa Aurora, built at the crossroads of

CENTRO DIREZIONALE, PERUGIA, MODEL OF THEATRE AND CULTURAL CENTRE

This concept of *frammenti* and fragmentation comes out in Aldo Rossi's drawings, where elements are culled from a wide variety of places, his own buildings and those of the past, real places and recollections of images evoked. These exploratory sketches together with formal designs, models and photographs of executed works shown in the exhibition *Aldo Rossi: Architect* reveal the relationship between new and old, design and building, the complex inter-reaction between a project in theory and execution, the elements that are built and those that remain on paper.

'*Cara architettura*', Aldo Rossi is both a

the resulting buildings speak of a unity of form, rather than eclecticism, because he removes the unnecessary and ephemeral. His architecture is in the tradition of Loos as well as early Palladio and the Italian vernacular. A methodical purpose and exploration links his projects, small changes and shifts in proportion give his work continuity and protection from passing fashion.

New architecture must involve a dialogue betwen the project and history and the city. New forms are subject to the involuntary memory of the city. Rossi does not believe in monolithic urban planning, but the evolution of cities that

Corso Emilia and Corso Giulio Cesare, the angled corner tower is sympathetic to the shape of the earlier building it faces across Corso Giulio Cesare. The side facades punctured by regular small windows flanked by the taller plain brick towers, and the uncluttered geometric form give the building solidity, and the stark columned entrance is a motif familiar from other projects, such as the broken corner with massive single column in his housing for IBA in Berlin. For the Casa Aurora Rossi takes up the classical hierarchy in the use of stone-facing for the first storey and the arcaded shops at ground level, with warm-coloured bricks for the upper levels. A simple cornice decoration divides and defines the two sections. Similarly, the windows on the lower section are square and set flush into the facade, those of the upper section more vertical and deeper set. Rossi views Turin as one of the most architecturally unified of Italian cities and has deliberately used local bricks and stone to fit into the Torinese tradition.

In the restoration and extension at De Amicis School at Bromi, 1969-70, Rossi aimed to set up a dialectic between the original building and the new construction, whereas to merely preserve is a false embalming process leading to the even-

–the dialectic betwen universal and particular forms. Rossi sees Venice as the ultimate man-made city, where man has transformed nature, yet it is also part of the littoral zone, the area between delta and sea, the place where the land ends and the sea begins. Its structural traditions, as with the Atlantic sea-faring nations Portugal and Britain, thus include the maritime and mercantile. The Teatro del Mondo referred to the Venetian tradition of shipbuilding as well as the historical 16th-century precedent of temporary pavilions, that temporarily alter the city landscape. The floating building was constructed of wooden panelling around a

ways, not just in the antique and official sense, but in the sense that important private buildings in an urban context become public, affecting those who live, work or pass-by. 'A grand building', he has said, 'is one of quality as well as size.' 'In a public city tolerance of the private is at a minimum.' In public works the architect must avoid imposing his own private, emotional, irrational self or personal 'style' but must strive to reveal the truth. 'Casa Aurora, like all important things and such I believe it is, was born out of a collaboration of many people; all those who have worked on this construction. This collaboration, from the designers in

Photos: Luigi Ghirri

SAN CATALDO CEMETERY, MODENA, *ABOVE*: PERSPECTIVE VIEW; *BELOW*: NOCTURNAL VIEW OF ENTRANCE; THE OSSUARY IN WINTER

tual decomposition of architecture and townscape. Even in his recent scheme for the restoration of the Carlo Felice Theatre in Genoa, 1982, where he decided Barabino's Neo-Classical facade must be reconstructed, the interior was to be a new creation, incorporating a reinterpretation of his familiar conical tower to provide light and space reaching up through the building.

The Teatro del Mondo for the 1980 Venice Biennale, further explored the dialectic between new and old and, in the ability to tow it around the Venetian lagoon and even across the Adriatic – and thus see the same structure in different settings

steel frame welded to a barge. Its octagonal form evoked memories of Italian baptistries, Shakespearian theatres and reappears in the theatre that forms the geometrical centre of a square, garden-courtyard of the Secondary School at Broni, which Rossi was designing prior to and during the Teatro del Mondo.

For Rossi architecture is public and is revealed in the city. It reflects his interest in the primary, essential, rational truth over irrational, personal style. In large public projects the architecture must adapt itself to the city, both as memory, entailing time, and as present. It is possible to talk of civic architecture in many

the studio to the bricklayers who carried out the work, is . . . one of the finest . . . things in architecture.' In social housing for Berlin one must resolve the problem of housing that is public where it meets the city whilst leaving the residents a degree of privacy and freedom of organisation.

The Centro Direzionale in Perugia, 1982-7, was conceived as a unified scheme, both public and private, with its combination of housing, office, storage, civic and cultural facilities. A large housing block on one side of a sloping Piazza faces a large civic building in the form of an arcaded *broletto* round three sides of a square courtyard, and at the head of the

Piazza, the cultural centre and theatre in the form of a rectangular block linked to a conical tower.

Rossi's work shows that classicism need not be the antithesis of the Modern, but can *be* modern. Rossi's classicism is one of austerity and proportion, it emphasises the rationality of essential generic forms and the relation between the parts, not decoration and ornament or an eclectic dislocation of elements. Rossi is interested in spatial volumes and like Loos, who he much admires, he eschews superfluous ornament for clarity and simple geometry. One of the earliest examples of this was the San Cataldo Cemetery at Modena,

style has been transported in this case to the islands of south Japan, although other recent projects have been for places as diverse as Berlin, Buenos Aires and Miami.

Essential classical elements have an independence so that they can be subtly repeated and metamorphosed, reappearing on different scales and for different purposes, from Alessi coffee pots, bathing cubicals and garaging to grand pedimented gables. A similar tower is used as an interior in the Genoa project and as a tower in the plans for the Congressional Palace in Milan and emerges in conical form in Perugia. Architecture is not re-

the known and the unknown.'

Aldo Rossi has recently been the subject of the exhibition, Aldo Rossi: Architect, *shown in late 1987 at York City Art Gallery*

 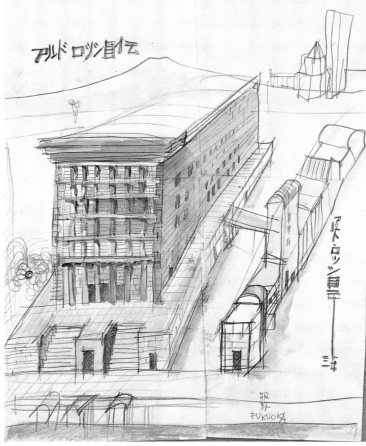

HOTEL IN FUKUOKA, JAPAN, *L TO R:* FRONT ELEVATION WITH WINDOWLESS OPENINGS; SKETCH OF HOTEL COMPLEX

dominated by the primary cubic form of the Ossuary, the shrine to the dead, a pure cube surrounded by the arcaded perimetal building. This cemetery has been a long-term project being built in stages since the initial competition in 1971. Recent photographs show the current stage of construction.

Another recent building is the hotel at Fukuoka in Japan, where windowless openings have been used to metamorphose the at first sight traditional classical facade of the front elevation and give articulation to what is in reality a solid wall. Universal forms and local context are combined so that his seemingly very Italian

lated merely to place and function but to architecture. Of his method Rossi has said: 'different things shed light upon one another or take on a different light when brought together – in other words, to analogy or to any other comparison that increases our capacity for understanding.' Luigi Ghirri, who has for many years taken photographs of Rossi's executed buildings, has described how they have continued to amaze him 'not because they belonged to the category of the unusual or the abstruse, but because they appeared immediately familiar and yet mysterious. They formed a singular fusion of the rediscovered and the never-before-seen,

and in early 1988 at RIBA in London. We are grateful to the Italian Embassy and Umberto Vattani, Minister for the Embassy, who have promoted this exhibition as a mark of the continuance today of the long tradition of Anglo-Italian cultural relations, the Lord Mayor of York for his hospitality, Umberto Barbieri and Alberto Ferlenga for information and photographs of recent works and for permission to reproduce material from the exhibition catalogue published by Electa Spa of Milan, and Isabella Ragattolla and the directors of Gruppo Finanzario Tessile for material on Casa Aurora, and naturally, above all, we should like to thank Aldo Rossi.

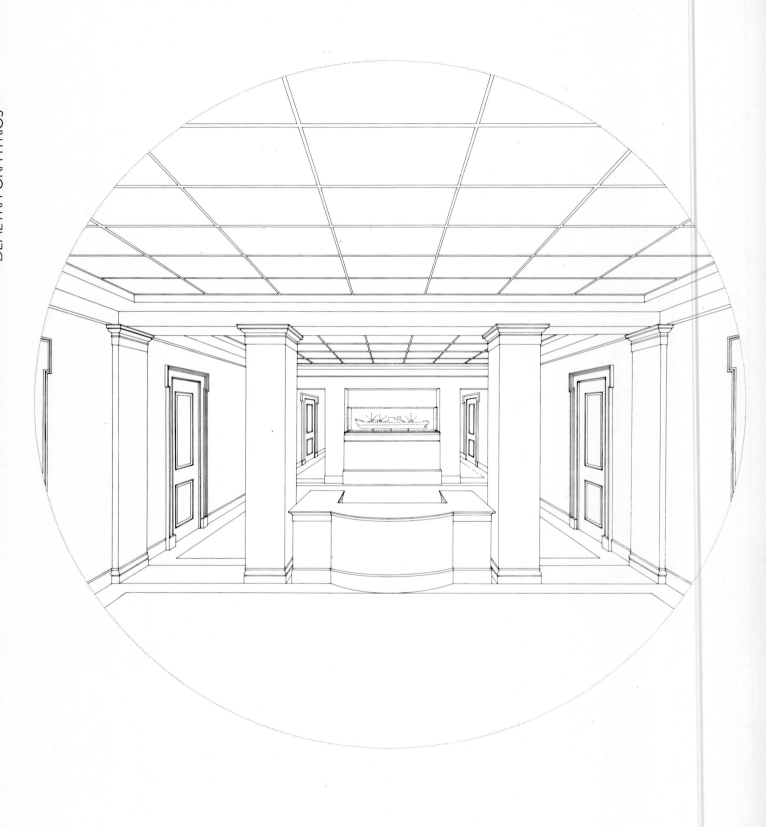

RECEPTION HALL

DEMETRI PORPHYRIOS
Shipping Offices, City of London, 1987

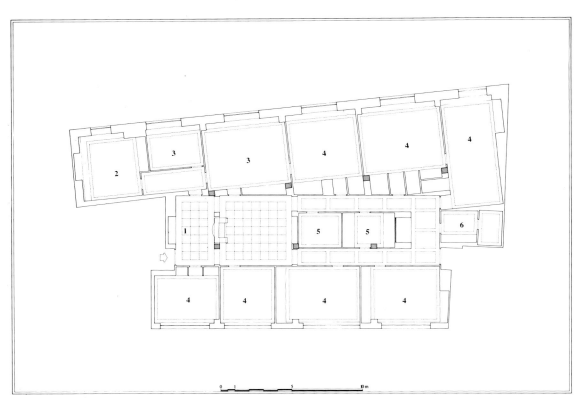

FLOOR PLAN
1 RECEPTION HALL 2 BOARDROOM 3 DIRECTORS' SUITE
4 GENERAL OFFICES 5 TELEX ROOMS 6 ANCILLARY

The offices are for a firm of shipbrokers in the City of London. The client was unhappy with the open plan of the building he had just acquired and requested a cellular re-organisation of space.

We had to work within an existing, geometrically irregular envelope, in which the columns of the concrete frame followed the converging long elevations of the building. Our first concern, therefore, was to devise a system of *poché* that would house the ancillary, storage and service requirements, and at the same time mediate between the peculiarities of the existing geometry. We thus transformed the incidental and the haphazard into a sequence of constituted rooms.

The offices are organised along the two long elevations of the building, opening either onto the central reception hall or the telex and communications core. Fitted cupboards and storage spaces for every office are accommodated in the *poché* so that the habitable space of the office is left unencumbered. The clarity of each room

Photo: Richard Cheatle

OFFICE FURNITURE

is emphasised by a border in the carpet and by the central light grid in the ceiling. This light grid reads as a roof light and articulates the otherwise unadorned junction between ceiling and wall with a perimeter lintel and a ceiling border. In the reception hall the same light grid is repeated, but on a grand scale.

The perimeter of the ceiling light grids has been specially designed to house the outlets of the ventilation and air-conditioning systems. Heating is by means of fan-coil units along the external walls.

All doors, architraves, skirtings and fitted office cupboards are specially made in light-grey stained oak, as is all the furniture, including office desks, tables, chairs and sofas, which the client also asked us to design. The joinery work in the directors' suite is made in eucalyptus wood, naturally stained and polished.

Project Team: Demetri Porphyrios, Alireza Sagharchi; *Services Engineers*: Max Fordham & Partners; *Building Contractors*: Morgan Lovell Ltd

51

INTERIOR VIEWS

INTERIOR VIEWS

IÑIGUEZ & USTARROZ
Two Projects for Lesaka

MEDICAL CENTRE, *CLOCKWISE FROM TOP LEFT*: ROOF DETAIL; VIEW; BRONZE SERPENT BY IMANOL ARRIAGA AGUIRRE; COURTYARD

The Medical Centre 1982-7

The Medical Centre is built on a courtyard that is closed on three sides, opening on the fourth through a pergola. A solid block base ensures the building's foundations and absorbs the slope of the terrain. With the exception of the base and pergola, the building is entirely rendered. The courtyard is composed of four concave flowerbeds with a sculpted bronze serpent at the centre. A cloister gallery links the various parts of the centre: entrance, waiting room, consultation and treatment rooms, service and emergency areas. A small tower acts as a counterpoint to the composition of the courtyard.

Restoration of the Town Hall 1981-7

A refurbishment, more than any other type of project, forces the architect to come to terms with architecture of the highest order. It is without doubt the quintessence of the art of designing, the remoulding of an architecture thrown into *discordantia partium* through ruin, alteration, destruction, changes in use.

The subject of this refurbishment was Lesaka Town Hall, a fine example of a late-Baroque palace dating from the end of the 18th century. Its exterior was in remarkably good condition, with the handsome stonework facades and large overhanging roof remaining intact. The interior, however, had been much altered, most detrimentally by the displacement of the main staircase.

To restore the lost harmony of the building, the missing portions of party walls were rebuilt and the recent, injudicious partitioning of rooms reversed. The most important element of the project, however, was the recreation of the central stairway. With this in its original position, the palace can regain the character of a public building. Made of oak, with decorative detailing in copper, the stairway is situated around a small court and crowned by a stucco cupola and lantern.

M Iniguez & A Ustarroz

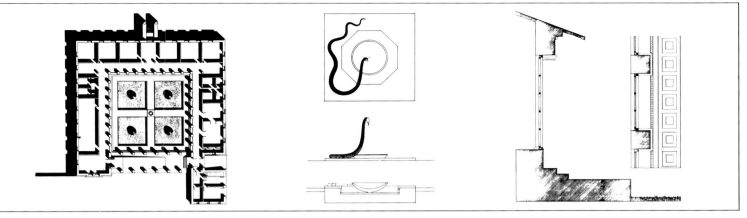

MEDICAL CENTRE, *L TO R:* GROUND PLAN; DESIGN FOR SNAKE FOUNTAIN; SECTION THROUGH WALL

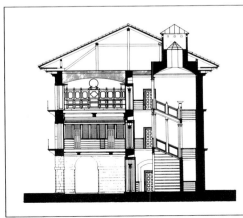

TOWN HALL, *L TO R:* DETAILS; *CENTRE:* SKETCH OF INTERIOR

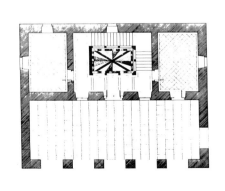

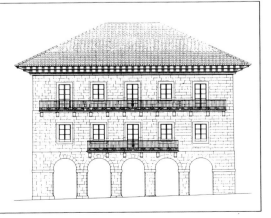

TOWN HALL, *L TO R:* CROSS SECTION; GROUND PLAN; ELEVATION

55

CARL LAUBIN, *OPENING DAY*, 1987

LEON KRIER
Atlantis, Tenerife

CARL LAUBIN, *ATLANTIS AT SUNRISE*, 1987

THE ARCHITECT'S CATEGORICAL IMPERATIVE

freely interpreted from IK

Build in such a way that the concept of your design is valid as a principle of both architecture and urbanism.

Build in such a way that you and your loved ones can find pleasure at any time in using your buildings, looking at them, living, working, holidaying and growing old in them.

LK

APPROACH TO THE AGORA FROM ARONA, HOTEL DRIVE

Atlantis is an international place of encounter and research for the arts, sciences, politics and business promoted by H J Müller. It will be built in Tenerife and completed by the year 2000. The project, including drawings, paintings, watercolours and models, is on show in a travelling exhibition which started its tour at the German Architecture Museum in Frankfurt am Main in December 1987.

Atlantis: A Tour of the City
The site for Atlantis is a terraced southeasterly slope with wonderful views of the ocean some 5 km away. In plan, as well as silhouette, the city describes a roughly pyramidal figure, whose base is the Corniche Promenade 595m above sea level and apex the church at 635m. In the centre of this triangle, lying some 618m above sea level at the foot of the Acropolis (high city), is the Agora (marketplace), which is bounded on one side by the small mountain road between Arona and San Miguel. The stone podium of the Agora dominates both the city below and the surrounding landscape.

The new community truly turns its face towards the rising sun. The silvery morning light is particularly pleasant and the late afternoon sun, instead of blinding you, models the landscape.

The usual practice with projects the size of Atlantis is to incorporate everything in one single building, literally under one roof, with a single entrance. This results in rambling and labyrinthine complexes which, independent of function and form, almost invariably come across as oppressive, confusing, depressing and overpowering. The effect, in other words, is institutional and inhuman.

In Atlantis, on the other hand, the programme is split up into more than a hundred buildings, both large and small, each of which can be simplified to its typologically irreducible core: church, baths, gallery, library, theatre, restaurant, workshop, house, etc. These building types represent the hierarchic components of the city.

With the exception of the 'Great Tower', all the buildings are only one or two storeys tall, although their heights vary considerably according to their use and significance. The *one-storey* church is, for example, 50m high, whilst some *two-storey* houses are only 8m.

Whilst there are very few internal passages and staircases, there are some 31 external streets, alleyways and stairways, and 19 squares, some small, others large. The streets are lined with plain-fronted houses, garden walls and pergolas, whereas on the squares are located communal buildings of a monumental charac-

ATRIUM CARRÉE, WITH THE FOUNDERS' NAMES INSCRIBED ON SIDE WALLS

ter which both qualify and dominate the lines of sight within the city. The houses are on the narrowest alleys, but they all have a garden terrace with a view of the countryside. The great number and extent of alleys, streets and paths (4.5km over the 5-hectare site) permits the richest variety on the minimum space.

The Acropolis
The 42m-high 'Great Tower' and the four-towered 'Atrium Carrée' form the propylaea to the upper city, framing the stairs which lead from the Agora up to the church. In the 17m-climb, the width of the stairs tapers in a forced perspective from 25m to 2m.

The art museum consists of 17 separate pavilions built on top of 4 man-made terraces which house storerooms, restoration labs, a parking garage and administrative offices, as well as the artificially lit exhibition rooms.

There is no prescribed route for going around the museum. The pavilions are self-contained works of art whose form is determined by the type of space within them (long gallery, stepped hall, etc). They are differentiated from each other both spatially and formally – narrow, high, deep, wide, stepped, light, dark – but architecturally they all speak the same language. The transition from the tempered interiors into the dazzling light outside is eased by porticos and arcades. Here, alleys and squares play the role of musical intervals. The exhibited artworks will, together with the buildings, create unique places. The presence of nature, the range of views out into the countryside and over the rooftops, create a relaxed, unhurried atmosphere, rather than one of forced self-cultivation.

The brightness of the picture galleries contrasts sharply with the enveloping darkness inside the church. The naves of the Greek Cross are 4m wide and 48m high. Only a little light is allowed to percolate into the interior through 2cm-wide vertical slits. The altar is raised on 7 steps in the transept.

The 'Atrium Carrée' opens out onto the landscape along the full breadth of its court-yard. Set under its 13m-wide archway is a sealed bronze shrine containing a record of the founding of the city: the names of its founders are inscribed in the flanking blind arches.

The 'Great Tower' is crowned by a 7m-high belvedere with a wide, projecting balcony. Underneath it are an artist's studio, the director's apartment and offices; below at the level of the upper square, is a *tapas* bar with seating spread out in the shade of the two open porticos.

EARLY SPRING SKY, COLOUR DRAWING BY RITA WOLFF, 1987

THE AGORA OF ATLANTIS, COLOUR DRAWING BY RITA WOLFF, 1987

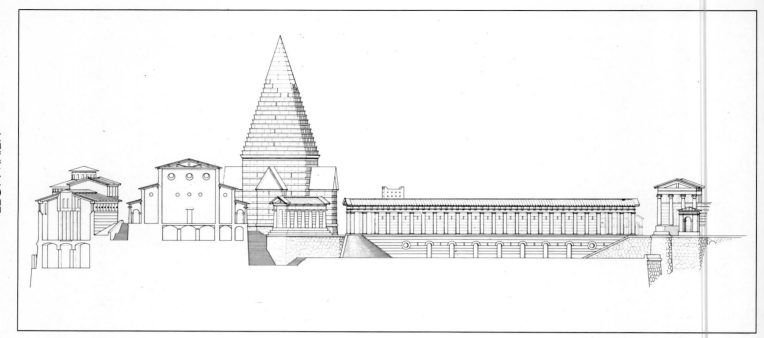

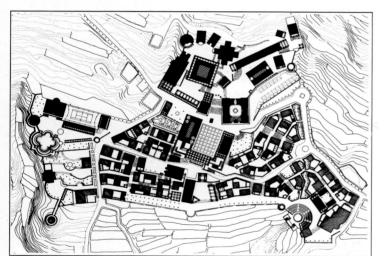 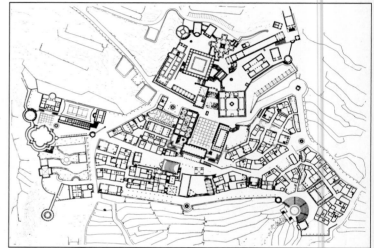

ABOVE L TO R: ELEVATION OF ART MUSEUM, CHURCH, LONG GALLERY; *BELOW L TO R:* SITE PLAN, GROUND FLOOR PLAN

The Agora

The Agora sits like a bastion on an overhang 618m above sea level. The 24-columned stoa (open market hall) stands between the square and the open countryside, but the transparency of its colonnades allows views as far as the sea. The high, covered terraces of the restaurant also link the square with the countryside on their southeastern edge. Opposite is the hotel reception which is grouped with a number of small shops around a covered arcade. The hotel drive is located further west in a landscaped square with a fountain. The square overlooks the herb garden like a terrace. The connecting road to the lower part of the city runs parallel to the Corniche Promenade below the Agora at 604m above sea level. This is where the facilities requiring delivery of heavy goods and instruments are located: work-

shops, a printer, sculptor's studio and pottery, the refectory kitchen and so on.

The Houses and Studios

45 houses and 11 studios, each with a garden terrace, comprise the real fabric of the city to the left and right of the main axis. The houses are of 5 basic types: linear, L-shape, L+tower, tower, polygon.

The Hanging Gardens

The spherical vessel on top of the heating plant marks the westernmost point of the town. The hanging gardens run from here along the steeply sloped *baranco* up to the bathing, sport and spa centre. While the terrace of the 20m² cloverleaf swimming pool dominates the ravine, the tennis courts are sheltered by the baths, fitness centre and laboratory building. A palm grove flanks the open, round gymnasium

hall, which has a tea bar at its plinth. Together with the podium of the baths, this area provides a protected solarium around the swimming pool.

The Corniche Promenade

The 350m-long Corniche Promenade marks the lower boundary of Atlantis. This is where people meet for their evening *paseo*. The promenade broadens, at the point where it bisects the city axis, into a square which contains the large refectory, a grotto, fountains and open porch. At its eastern end, the street terminates in a semi-circular open-air theatre, whose cavea is dominated by the tympanum of the library and flanked by a small music studio and monopteros.

Topography and the Form of the City

The form and fabric of the city were largely

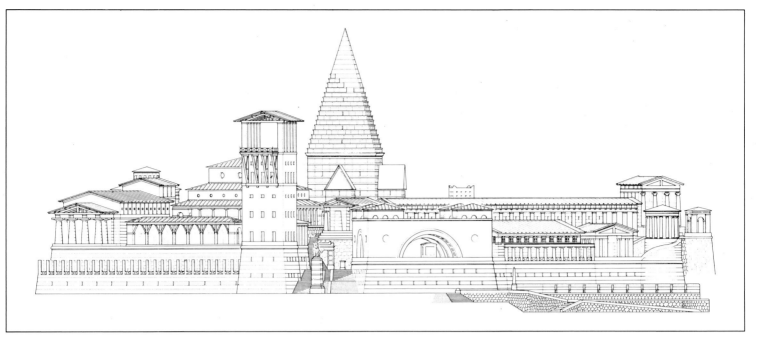

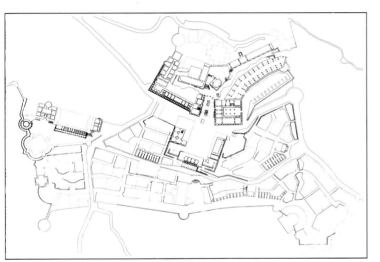 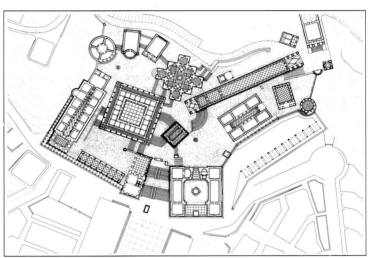

ABOVE: SOUTH ELEVATION OF ACROPOLIS; *BELOW L TO R:* PLAN SHOWING TERRACES AND UNDERGROUND BUILDINGS, PLAN OF ACROPOLIS

determined by the topographic configuration of the site. The cavea of the theatre, the terraces of the hanging gardens and the large podia of the Agora and the Acropolis all simply accentuate the natural topography. Respect for these features, combined with a complete freedom from the grid, makes the form of the city naturally fluid. The methods used here are the same as those proven in the creation of the great cities of the past.

Nowadays picturesque street patterns and organic urban structures are frequently thought to have grown as unconsciously as flowers in a field. People like to forget that the plasticity, perspective and symbolic precision of these apparently freely formed stone masses are not the fortuitous product of a spontaneous zeal for building but represent, on the contrary, the attainment of the highest sense

of ordering, the realisation and consolidation of the highest ethical and artistic consciousness.

It is the organic quality in the order of historic cities which points the way out of dull expressionism on the one hand and mechanical schematicism on the other.

Building Technique and Appearance
Only traditional methods and materials will be used in the building of Atlantis, although they will of course be combined with the most up-to-date tools and technical equipment. The large terraces are built with ashlar, the smaller ones with quarrystones. In Tenerife the stonemason's craft is still very much alive, as can be seen in the construction of the massive retaining walls of the vast new plantations. The houses are made of whitewashed quarrystones. The roofs have

wooden carpentry and are covered with terracotta tiles. The monumental buildings are constructed in a similar way, but with the addition of architectural elements such as columns, door and window-lintels, balustrades and cornices of massive quarrystones such as granite and travertine. Some of the roofs are covered with sheet copper, others with vitreous green tiles.

Architectural elements and mouldings are used sparingly, and then only in monumental buildings, fountains, street furniture, etc.

This architecture will convey the impression of solid craftsmanship, archaic solidity, and simple elegance.

Assistants: Robert Day, Janusz Maciag.

THE ACROPOLIS OF ATLANTIS, COLOUR DRAWING BY RITA WOLFF, 1987

DEMETRI PORPHYIOS
A Critique of Atlantis

LEON KRIER

The Post-Modern fascination with history and the past is not sustained by the nostalgia of homecoming. The past is seen not as a paradigm but as an aesthetic of voyeurism observing 'clandestinely the pleasure of others'. But while the 'darkness of exile flows from forgetfulness', it is 'in remembrance that the secret of life lies.' Surely this is a very different vision of the world. Here we find people for whom the old words count and remain true. Remembering, recognising the familiar, interpreting, speaking, building a home, all begin to countervail loss and orient the desire to redeem that loss.

Such is the significance of classicism today. Such is the contribution of Leon Krier's work. Such is the aim of the masterplan for Atlantis. Surely this is not the utopian city of the fable but a real plan for a town where the classical values of order and clarity are emphasised.

What is the urban structure of Atlantis? First of all this is a finite town with clearly marked boundaries which distinguish urban life from the countryside. This is an important critique of the present-day sprawl of cities and of the attendant destruction of both the city and the countryside. Krier is highlighting the necessity for such a distinction as a prerequisite for the recuperation of the pleasures of urban life and the countryside alike.

The urban structure of Atlantis is at the same time both simple to grasp and rich in spatial and symbolic implications. The town is organised along two main axes. The north/south axis is orthogonal to the contours of the land and organises the public buildings of the museum complex, the church, restaurants, marketplace and dining halls. Through the sweeping vista that both frames and embraces the countryside it relates the upper with the lower city. The upper city is rendered in the image of an acropolis: a number of free-standing museum buildings and the church speak of the occasion of the city's founding. This is a model town where patrons, artists, scientists, philosophers and connoisseurs have come together with a common goal: unlike the engineering aims of the St Simonians, theirs is a revival of humanism.

The lower city unfolds along the east/west axis and follows the contours of the land. Here are the villas, studios and workshops flanked on one side by the library and theatre and on the other by the health and sports buildings. The symbolic implications are unequivocal; the town proper is flanked by public buildings dedicated to the nourishment of the body and the mind. The streets that lead to those buildings, however, slide past one another and are united only at their confluence with the north/south axis; an axis that celebrates the relationship between nature and the representation of nature in the form of an acropolis of art.

Laterally, the lower city is bound by three main routes. Along the edges of the acropolis runs the main street. This is the main approach into and out of Atlantis. It is a country road that winds uphill affording the visitor panoramic or framed views of the town and is the only place where the acropolis and the lower town meet spatially. The second lateral route collects the flow of the small paths around which the villas and studios are organised. The third lateral route, the Corniche, forms the southern boundary of the town and is treated as a leisurely boulevard and a *belvedere* from which to sample the joys of the *campagna* beyond.

I have spoken of axes but it should be remembered that there are no straight lines in Atlantis. On the contrary, with the exception of the central town square, the open spaces are always non-geometrical figures designed to be appreciated perspectively. The rigid lines of the functionalist planner have given way here to a multitude of highly individualised spaces. The buildings (whether villas, studios or public buildings) are always simple geometrical volumes; the scale, construction and decoration of which point clearly to their use and civic hierarchy. No building corner or facade, no terrace or pergola or winding path has been placed accidentally. They have all been studied as perspectival tableaux where framed vistas and framing elements partake of an incessant symbolic exchange. It is exactly the elocution of these perspectival tableaux which carries us forward as we walk through the varied streets of Atlantis.

Measured against the aesthetics of voyeurism of contemporary Post-Modern and Neo-Modern cultures, classicism appears the only critical and progressive stance to take. This is so since the indiscriminate historicism of Post-Modernism or the pseudo-scientism of Modernism have disembodied both the city and its architecture. The crudity of Modernism and Post-Modernism alike has been their inability to embrace those humanist values which make individuals into citizens.

Many 'cultivated' people today, however, look at classicism with an air of condescension. At best they are making a point of the fact that they cannot take classicism seriously. At worst, by accusing classicism of brutality and manipulatory tactics, they conclude that classicism is a regressive vision. The same 'cultivated' people are fascinated with baseball. At play, mob emotions are boiled in an open pot, so to speak. Let us not forget, however, that the gladiatorial combat owes its paroxysmic savagery not to the players (who are after all neutral) but to the audience who have the actual power of life and death over the people who are entertaining them. Similarly, there can be no communist, fascist or democratic windows. Associations are always protected by the convention of the form; but it is *us* who make those conventions and who can either break away from them or cling stubbornly to the shadow of a guilt complex as a ritual re-enactment of penance.

ACROPOLIS FROM THE AGORA

CLOS PEGASE WINERY, DETAILS OF INTERIOR AND EXTERIOR

MICHAEL GRAVES
Two Recent Projects

PUBLIC ENTRANCE FACADE

Clos Pegase Winery

The Clos Pegase Winery, in the Napa Valley of California, takes its name and thematic organisation from the myth of Pegasus, the subject of a significant painting by Odilon Redon in the owner's art collection. The project, in which Michael Graves collaborated with the New York artist, Edward Schmidt, includes: a winery with public winetasting and more private winemaking functions, a residence for the owner, and a public sculpture park for outdoor events and display of the owner's collection of sculpture. The winery and residence have been built as the first phase of the project.

The master plan organises the site along an axis of water emanating from the 'grotto of Pegasus' at the summit of the knoll, and ending with two formal ponds. The public activities of the winery and the sculpture garden are located on one side of the axis while the more private winemaking functions are located on the other side. Wine is stored in caves dug into the hillside. The residence, located on the 'private' side, is protected from public activities and enjoys views of the vineyards to the south and east. The winery building is organised in two main wings with separate entrances, although the symmetrical public facade gives it a unified image. The offices and public winetasting rooms are located in one wing, entered from a large public portico. The other wing includes the winemaking functions and is entered from the working court and delivery area.

The divisions in landscape and building are symbolic of the dual themes of the public and private, of the process of winemaking and pleasure of tasting.

Erickson Alumni Center

The Erickson Alumni Center, West Virginia University, is designed for alumni banquets, receptions, and meetings and also includes the offices of the West Virginia University Alumni Association. Located on a sloping site on a college road at the edge of the campus, the Center is developed on two levels. Built into the slope of the hillside are two storeys of offices and meeting rooms overlooking a double height banqueting hall, which opens on to a large terrace for outdoor events. In character, the Alumni Center is seen as a large house, an inviting and familiar place for alumni returning to the campus. Elements such as the dormers, the fireplace and chimney, and the garden lattice help establish the domestic character of the architecture.

ERICKSON ALUMNI CENTER, DETAILS OF INTERIOR AND EXTERIOR

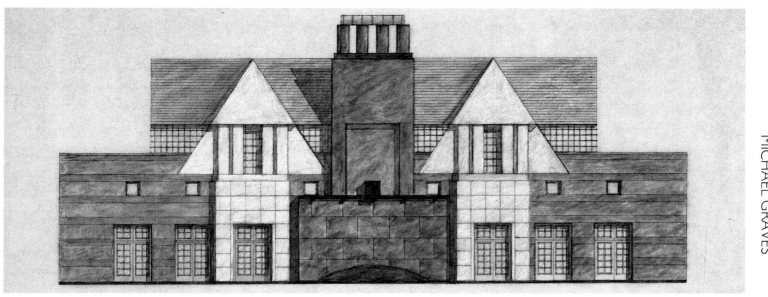

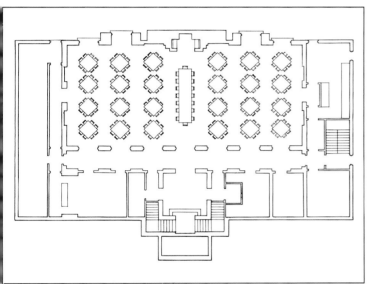

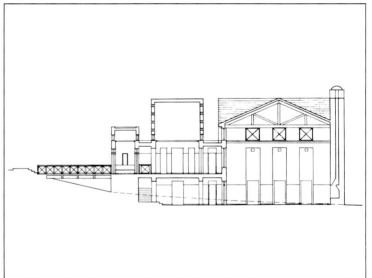

ABOVE AND BELOW: GARDEN ELEVATION; *CENTRE*: GROUND FLOOR PLAN AND TRANSVERSE SECTION

STREET ELEVATION

DEMETRI PORPHYRIOS
House in Kensington, 1987

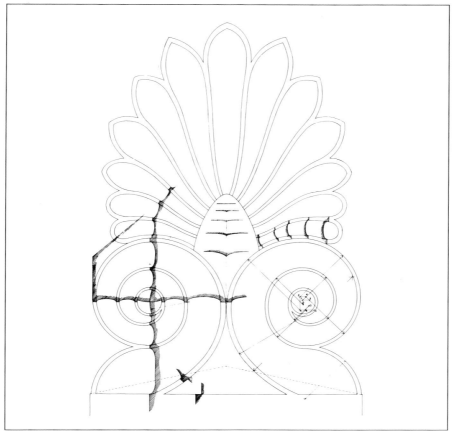

DETAIL OF ANTHEMION

his is a new house in a residential area of ensington. The existing dilapidated uilding was taken down and the client ked us to design a five-storey single mily house.

The terraces in the street generally date om the late 18th and early 19th centuries. s a whole, they are well maintained with e occasional extension or refurbishment. hile there are also a couple of Arts and rafts insertions in the street, its overall aracter is established by the Neo-lassical treatment of the architecture.

As is expected of terraced houses, the te is rather restricted and has a frontage nine metres. Early in the design we ecided to maintain the planimetric rganisation typical of these houses. aterally, the building is organised in two nequal bays. This is a sensible and time-onoured solution, since by grouping cir-lation and ancillary spaces along the arrow bay the rest of the frontage is eed for reception rooms.

Traditionally, the staircase connects all

the floors, and does not establish a distinction between the more public reception areas and the private bedrooms. But in this project, taking into account the size of the house, we felt it was necessary to make this distinction. This we achieved by differentiating both spatially and figuratively between the entrance hall staircase and the oval staircase situated next to the lift and used by the family on a daily basis.

The entrance hall staircase is housed in a room of its own, measuring seven metres in height and connecting the library and dining room with the main reception rooms of the first floor. At ground floor the library connects with the dining room, which in turn opens out on to a terrace overlooking the garden. Guests can have direct access to the glazed conservatory by means of the oval staircase. Also at garden level are the family room, kitchen and all the ancillary and service spaces. The first floor is taken up mostly by the master bedroom suite. Here the master bedroom, dressing room and master

bathroom are organised in an *enfilade* fashion that reveals the full depth of the house while avoiding any axial emphasis.

The first floor is devoted entirely to the drawing room. This connects visually with the double space of the entrance hall by means of three internal windows. At this floor the full extent of the house is revealed, and it is here that the floor to ceiling height is the most generous, measuring almost four metres.

The tripartite articulation of the street elevation into rusticated base, *piano nobile* and attic top is marked by the prominent cornice that crowns the *piano nobile* and by the elaboration of the window architraves that correspond to the drawing room and the entrance hall.

At the rear elevation, the tower of the oval staircase, the conservatory and the family room project from the main volume of the house and are treated in an additive manner. The pilasters and glazed intercolumniations at garden level act as a base on top of which the house proper is articu-

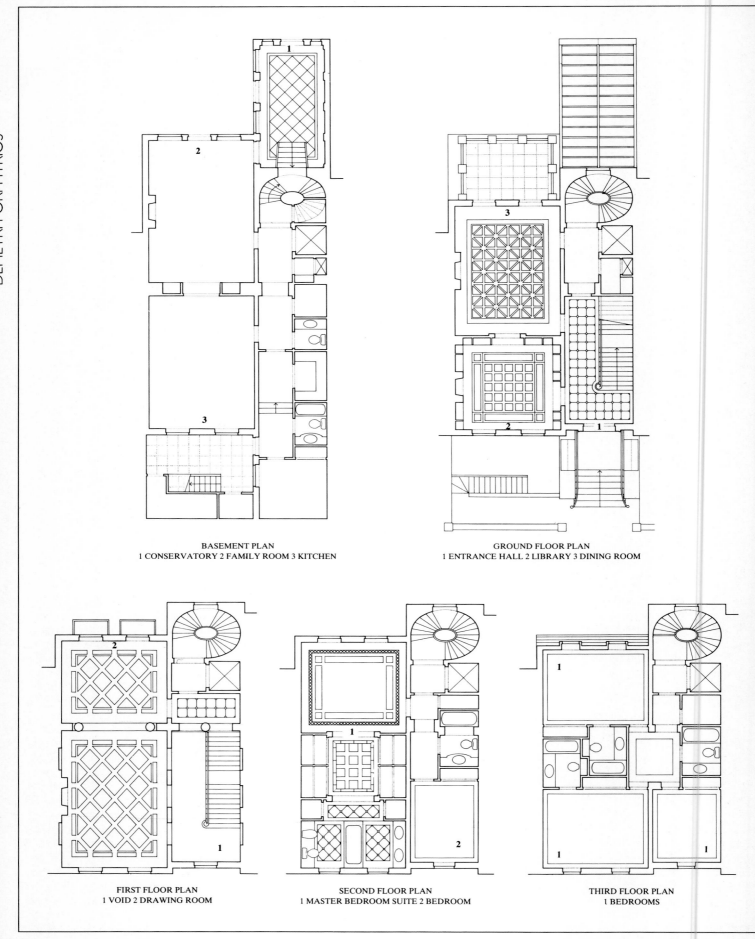

BASEMENT PLAN
1 CONSERVATORY 2 FAMILY ROOM 3 KITCHEN

GROUND FLOOR PLAN
1 ENTRANCE HALL 2 LIBRARY 3 DINING ROOM

FIRST FLOOR PLAN
1 VOID 2 DRAWING ROOM

SECOND FLOOR PLAN
1 MASTER BEDROOM SUITE 2 BEDROOM

THIRD FLOOR PLAN
1 BEDROOMS

REAR ELEVATION

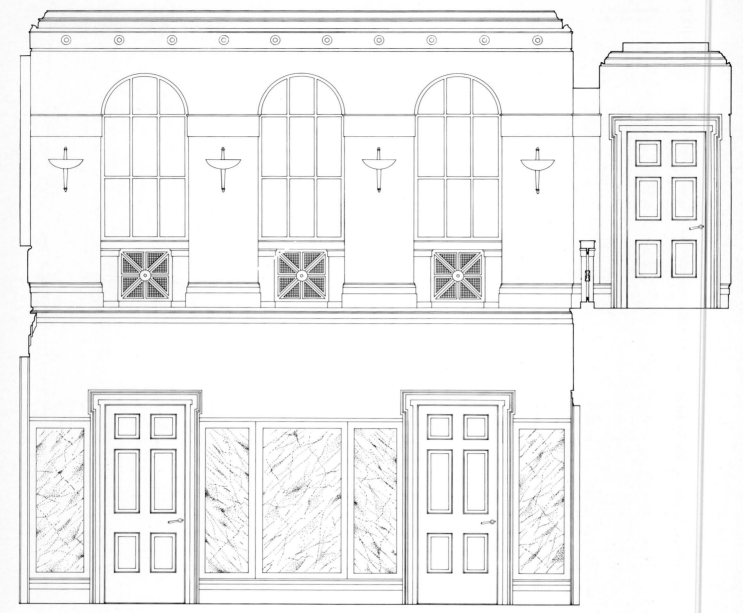

ENTRANCE HALL ELEVATION

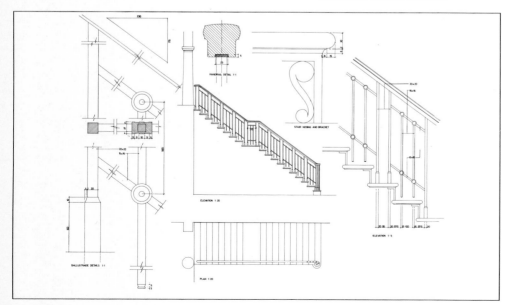

DETAIL OF STAIRCASE

lated in three parts crowned by a steep slated roof.

Externally, the street elevation is rendered and painted in off-white while the rear elevation is faced in brick, except for the projecting volumes at garden level which are rendered. The front steps are stone and all profiles to cornices, window architraves and diestones as well as the pedimented front entrance are formed *in situ* in render.

Internally, walls are plastered and are either painted or finished in stretched fabric. The entrance hall has a base in *stucco lustro* that is divided in painted panels of Pompeian red, with the rest of the walls in hues of ochre. Floors are finished in parquet for the reception rooms, carpet for the bedrooms, marble for the bathrooms and the conservatory, and stone for the entrance hall.

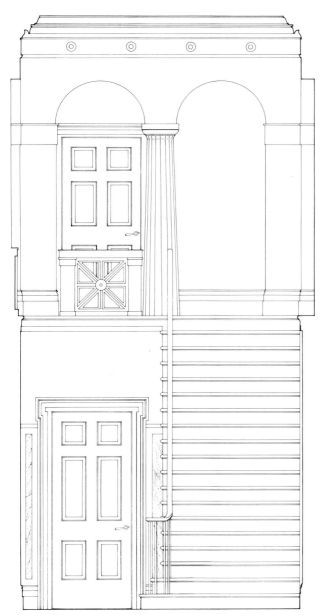

ENTRANCE HALL ELEVATION

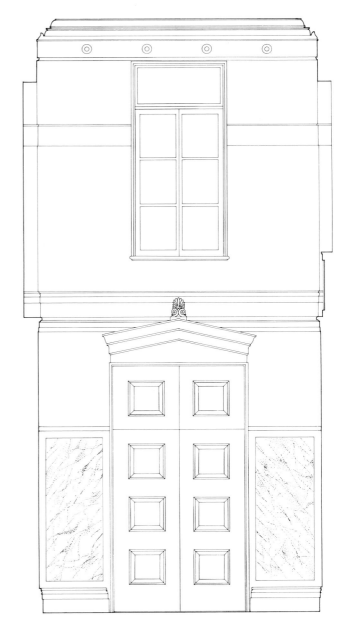

ENTRANCE HALL ELEVATION

All internal cornices, coffers and anthemia to the pediments have specially made profiles in fibrous plaster. The Doric columns are also specially designed and solidly made in hard plaster of Paris. In general all joinery, including architraves, skirtings, fielded and raised doors, windows as well as radiator casings, wardrobes and vanitory units, are custom-made in hardwood for painting. The panelling and bookcases for the library are in English oak stained and polished. We have also designed the light fittings for the entrance hall as well as all metalwork for railings internally and externally.

Project Team: Demetri Porphyrios, Alireza Sagharchi, Ian Sutherland, Liam O'Connor, Nigel Cox; *Structural Engineers:* Cameron Taylor Partners; *Client:* Balli Development Ltd

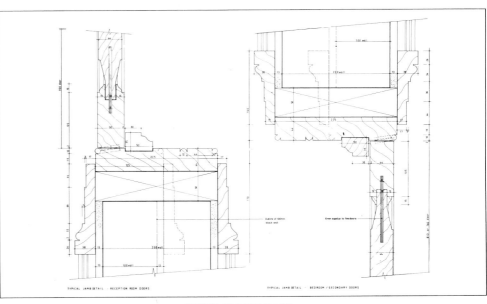

DETAIL OF DOOR JAMBS

DRAWING ROOM

LIBRARY

ENTRANCE HALL

WINDOW DETAIL

JAMES STIRLING
Science Centre, Berlin

Photo: David Rosie

SCIENCE CENTRE FROM NEW NATIONAL GALLERY SQUARE

Now nearing completion, the Science Centre occupies a significant site in the southern Tiergartenviertel district of Berlin. It is in the area of the Kulturforum with the new National Gallery by Mies van der Rohe and Hans Scharoun's Philharmonie building. James Stirling and Michael Wilford Associates designed the centre as a result of their prize-winning entry in the competition organised by IBA in 1979 and construction began in 1984.

The Centre is to house the social science research institutes – Environment Institute, Management Institute, Social Institute – at present spread out in various parts of the city, together with the offices of the central organisation. Facilities provided will include offices, meeting rooms, conference and lecture halls, a library, and more informal tea rooms and cafeterias.

The scheme required retension of the huge, ornate, 19th-century, Beaux Arts-style, former Law Courts building which overlooks the Landwehrkanal. This building, which was converted to house the Secretariat and general services, has a strong image and with the grand scale of its rooms would be hard to integrate in a simple extension, as the high rooms would not correspond to the new floor levels. The new buildings were therefore designed to be relatively independent, clustered around a central garden. They are linked to each other and the existing building by loggias and arcades and interconnect at every floor level. The individual components are in differing geometric forms and at varying scales to avoid the box-like banality of huge office blocks which Stirling sees as one of the most destructive features of post-war urban development. The most distinctive masses are the tall hexagonal form of the library – an eight-storey tower with the principal reading room on the ground floor and the book stacks on the upper levels easily reached by lifts – and the rotunda building with fan-shaped conference rooms. From the outside the rotunda is not unlike a stark Colosseum or Albert Hall, when approached from the interior court it presents a plain, white, concave facade.

Marked by the striped polychromy that has become so much a feature of Stirling's work of the 80s, in contrast to the red brick of the 60s, the lowest section of the walls have stone cladding, but above that the walls have been left in concrete, coloured in broad bands of soft pink and blue on alternating floors. A marked feature has been made of the projecting terracotta-coloured architraves of the windows which stand out in relief from the facades.

STIRLING & WILFORD
No 1, Poultry, Revised, City of London

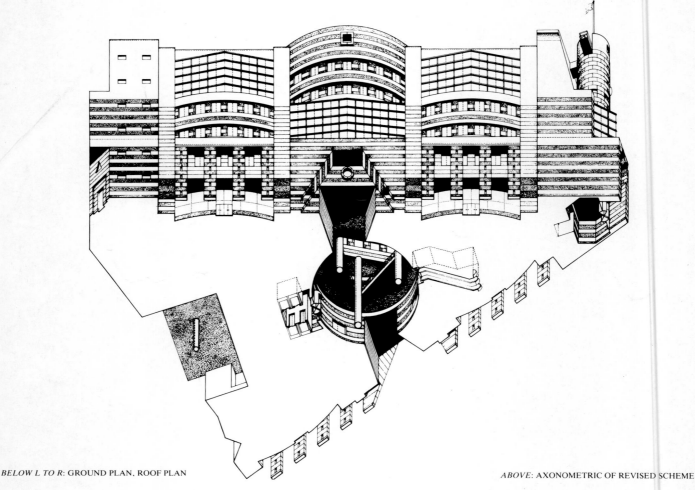

BELOW L TO R: GROUND PLAN, ROOF PLAN

ABOVE: AXONOMETRIC OF REVISED SCHEME

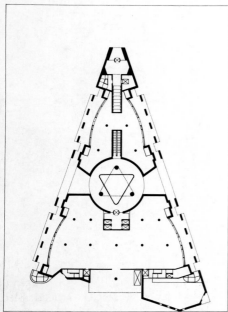

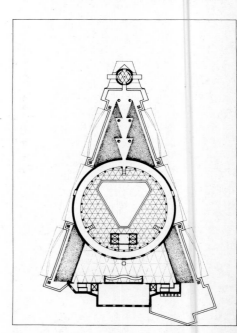

The second public inquiry for No 1 Poultry begins in May. The latest plans and axonometrics by Stirling, show refinement of the earlier design to produce a stronger, more articulated facade.

The corner tower has been made more prominent by separating it from the main form of the building at the upper levels. The facade bays have become more clearly defined through the reorganisation of office space to concentrate services in the perimeter, which has strengthened the vertical dividing elements. However, the horizontal polychromy has also been accentuated through the use of coloured sandstone banding and horizontal window mullions.

The pyramidal public entrances lead into a central lobby with gallery looking down into the basement and open, triangular light-well, which emerges at roof level in the raised circular roof garden.